A STORY OF QUINCY UNIVERSITY

Catholic, Franciscan, Beginning Again

THE FIRST 150 YEARS

BY JOSEPH ZIMMERMAN, O.F.M.

Fr. Erhard Kuester, O.F.M., who taught from 1940 until his death in 1968, exemplifies the "can-do" spirit of many of the earlier friars. He tried single-handedly to create an engineering program, and built, with donor support, an engineering building. Here he poses in that building with a group of his students. The picture is undated.

The Donning Company Publishers
184 Business Park Drive, Suite 206
Virginia Beach, VA 23462

Steve Mull, General Manager
Barbara Buchanan, Office Manager
Heather L. Floyd, Editor
Amanda Dawn Guilmain, Graphic Designer
Derek Eley, Imaging Artist
Debbie Dowell, Project Research Coordinator
Tonya Hannink, Marketing Specialist
Pamela Engelhard, Marketing Advisor

G. Bradley Martin, Project Director

Library of Congress Cataloging-in-Publication Data

Zimmerman, Joseph, 1935-
  A story of Quincy University : Catholic, Franciscan, beginning again : the first 150 years / by Joseph Zimmerman.
       p. cm.
  Includes index.
  ISBN 978-1-57864-572-5 (hardcover : alk. paper)
  1. Quincy University--History. 2. Catholic universities and colleges--Illinois--Quincy--History. 3. Franciscans--Illinois--Quincy. I. Title.
  LD4695.Z56 2010
  378.772'73--dc22
                        2009020069

Printed in the United States of America at Walsworth Publishing Company

Dedication

Joe Bonansinga had been a student at the College in the 1920s, where he took part in musical and dramatic productions. Throughout his long life, he was an enthusiastic supporter of the College as well as of the city of Quincy, which honored him with the title "Mr. Quincy" and named a street for him.

In the year 2000, Quincy University honored Joe Bonansinga with the title "Alumnus of the Century." He died in 2003.

"Alumnus of the Century,"
"Mr. Quincy," Joe Bonansinga,
1910–2003

This book is dedicated to his memory. He represents both the past and the future, as a layman who caught and lived the spirit of Francis and Clare of Assisi.

Table of Contents

Foreword

"You shall know the truth, and the truth shall set you free." (John 8:32)

THAT FAMOUS VERSE FROM JOHN'S GOSPEL IMMEDIATELY CAME TO MIND as I read the draft of Fr. Joe Zimmerman's history of Quincy University, written to commemorate the University's 150th anniversary. Fr. Joe's love for this institution shines through on every page, yet he never allows his affection to supersede his clarity as an historian and a sociologist.

Fr. Joe tells the truth about Quincy University, warts and all, past and present. From the "seraphic confusion" of its early Franciscan leaders to the Mississippi River flood, Fr. Joe recounts 150 years of the University's graced adventure—from its founding as a school for German immigrants on the eve of the Civil War, to the heyday of its growth a century later, to the turbulence of the decades following and to its present equilibrium, poised to move forward toward a challenging yet exciting future.

Through all its struggles, successes, and shortcomings, Quincy University has continued the great mission of educating students because of the countless faculty, staff, alumni, and friends who have loved and learned from her. Their enduring spirit—and their faith in the Spirit Who endures—continues to animate the campus and all those who study, work, and play here. Rooted in the service of the Franciscan Friars of Sacred Heart Province, the University's foundation is the Franciscan experience, especially the core values of hospitality and respect for all persons and all creation. There is a spirit of freedom at QU, grounded in the search for truth. Those are the values that will set the course for the future.

As Quincy University passes this exciting milestone en route to the next 150 years, we would do well to recall St. Francis's challenging words, taken from *The Life of St. Francis* by Thomas of Celano, and adopted by the Friars of Sacred Heart Province as the theme for their own sesquicentennial celebration in 2008:

"Let us begin to serve the Lord God, for up until now we have done little or nothing." Francis did not consider that he had already attained his goal, but tireless in the pursuit of holy newness, he constantly hoped to begin again.

The adventure of education is never complete. I hope you will enjoy Fr. Joe Zimmerman's fascinating tour through the first 150 years of Quincy University, and I hope you will join us for the adventure in the years to come.

Peace and all good,

Robert A. Gervasi, Ph.D.
President, Quincy University

Preface

FR. FRANCIS JEROME GRAY, O.F.M. TAUGHT HISTORY AT QUINCY COLLEGE from 1957 to 1989. He had received a doctorate in history from Fordham University and taught European history, focusing on Russian history, at Quincy College for thirty years. During that time, he also preached retreats, especially to groups of sisters. In his private life as a friar, he exemplified concern and care for the sick. He was beloved by students for his entertaining lectures, which featured emphasis on the humorous and outrageous behavior of historical figures, especially popes, priests, and empresses.

During his years here, Fr. "F.J." worked on a history of the College, writing and rewriting drafts of sections of the work and locating those drafts in loose-leaf binders which seem to be scattered all over the campus. His history ends with the year 1987.

In August of 2002, several years after he had been transferred from Quincy to Chicago, Fr. Francis Jerome gave a draft of his history to Drs. Barbara and John Schleppenbach, asking them to copy-edit the text. Barbara and John did just that, helped by a student named Edith Muyinda, transferring it to electronic media. The entire text was proofed again by Fr. Philibert Hoebing, a friar who has been at Quincy College since the early 1950s.

The text as Fr. Francis Jerome wrote it suffers from two deficiencies which make it in need of further editing before it can be published. One is his tendency to tell stories of individuals at whatever place in the text the story occurred to him, without regard to overall organization. Often he repeats a story or a statement. The other is his often casual approach to historical accuracy. He occasionally provides references that would enable one to verify his statements, but these citations are uneven in quality.

Fr. Francis Jerome Gray wrote a history of Quincy University on which much of this book is based. He was also a popular lecturer. In this 1986 photo he talks with, left to right, Patrick Newton, Brian O'Brien, Meagan Bain, and Mike Kenerly.

I have used his work as the basis for much of what I have written, and have tried not to repeat historical inaccuracies. My background is sociology, which has caused me to spend time collecting numbers from the College history, and to reflect on the sociological factors that have impacted the school's story.

Another friar, Fr. August Reyling, spent many hours compiling lists of all the students who ever registered at the College. His lists begin with the 1860 to 1870 classes, which are lumped together because there were no records of students in individual years, and continue to 1975. I have used those lists for comparisons, because they go back to the earliest days of the College, and because they represent a verifiable headcount for each year. Fr. August also compiled fact sheets on every man who entered Sacred Heart Province from 1859 to the present. The Provincial office in St. Louis continued the sheets after Fr. August retired.

I am grateful to Pat Tomczak for collecting older photographs from the University archives, to Greg McVey for photographs of athletic events, and to Mary Pat Vahlkamp for allowing me to browse in the files of the office of public relations. Fr. John Leonard Ostdiek provided me with pictures from his private collection.

Joseph Zimmerman, O.F.M.
Semi-retired Professor of Sociology, Quincy University

Introduction

THE FIRST CRITERION listed by the Higher Learning Commission (the Midwest agency that accredits colleges and universities) as the basis for evaluation of a school's worthiness of accreditation is the following:

> The organization operates with integrity to ensure the fulfillment of its mission through structures and processes that involve the board, administration, faculty, staff, and students.

The very earliest catalogs issued by the College, dated in the 1870s, describe three departments, with the following rationale—the first mission statement of the school:

> It is the object of the St. Francis Solanus College
>
> 1. To supply the deficiencies of an imperfect common school education (Preparatory)
>
> 2. To prepare young men for mercantile pursuits (Commercial)
>
> 3. To prepare students for such professional studies for which a classical course is either necessary or desirable (Classical)

These same three goals continued to appear in the catalogs of the College well into the twentieth century. The goals of the three programs grew out of a Franciscan tradition blending the ideals of St. Francis of Assisi with academic culture. The tradition began in the 1240s, when a master at the University of Paris, Alexander of Hales, became a Franciscan and continued teaching students who were Franciscan, most notably Bonaventure of Bagnoregio (St. Bonaventure).

One of the great scholars of Franciscan intellectual history, Fr. Philotheus Boehner, once listed four characteristics of a Franciscan approach to philosophy (and by implication, education): a Franciscan approach is critical (today we would use the phrase "critical thinking"); it is scientific (tending more toward empirical evidence than toward deductive reasoning); it is progressive (open to criticism and change); and it is practical (oriented toward the good of the student— "edifying" in the original meaning of the word, "building up").

The first friars came to Quincy at the request of the people of Quincy and the bishop of Alton, to respond to very practical interests. The people wanted their children to be educated, and the bishop wanted a place where his seminarians could study. The bishop's request was answered by Quincy College's sister college in Teutopolis, Illinois, and the people of Quincy got the school they wanted for their children (male children, of course—in the 1860s, girls did not go to most colleges).

Some of the Quincy students could not even read. The friars, then and now, assumed that if God sent a student to them, their job was to develop the student's abilities as much as possible in the time available, regardless of where the student was starting. This is the "practical" aspect of the tradition. It has continued in the reluctance of College authorities to reject students because they were not well prepared. This reluctance always has to be moderated by a concern for the welfare of better-prepared students, and by the creation of remedial programs for the less prepared. In contrast, Jesuit educational philosophy explicitly focuses on educating the elite of a society, both because *all* young people should be exposed to Gospel values (the rich need the Gospel too...), and because elites shape the culture and affect both rich and poor.

The "Commercial" program of the College answered the need of students to prepare themselves for employment—more evidence of the <u>practical</u> Franciscan approach. In contrast to more selective liberal arts schools, the College has always maintained curricula which we today call "professional."

However, the Commercial program in the early years was not "vocational" in today's sense. Here is the curriculum for the first year of the Commercial program in 1871:

Christian Doctrine
English, (grammar, reading, orthography, declamation)
German
Mathematics
History (Bible and U.S.)
Geography
Book-keeping
Natural philosophy
Drawing

In that list of subjects, Book-keeping is about the only one that we would label "vocational" today.

The "Classical" department contained pretty much the same list of subjects, with the addition of Latin, Greek, and French.

The combination of the goals of remediation, job preparation, and traditional liberal arts education have not always co-existed peacefully at the College. Over the years, friars and lay faculty have argued over whether the school should be a strictly liberal arts school, downplaying professional or Commercial programs. The argument for more exclusive liberal arts has never won out.

As Marshall Smelser, a student, commented in a 1935 editorial in the College newspaper, the *Falcon*:

It must be remembered that Quincy College students are not, in the main, students who go to college simply for the social prestige of the degree. Nearly all of them have a definite purpose in attending, and that purpose is chiefly one of professional preparation. Few come simply for the vaguely defined "cultural contacts" that characterize the student bodies of so many liberal arts colleges.

PLANNING AND THE LACK OF IT

In some ways, all human institutions exist without much planning, in the sense that the men and women who create them set out with many different ideas of what they want to do. Those ideas constantly change, are often the subject of serious disagreements and conflicts, and are shaped by the individual personalities of the people who make up the institution.

Quincy University has lacked systematic planning more than most other colleges and universities. Franciscans do indeed have a tradition of involvement in academic life, but they are also involved in many other activities. In the Province of the Sacred Heart, the Franciscan group that founded Quincy College, educators have comprised only about 10 percent of the membership. The majority of friars, both ordained and not ordained, have done parish work, because that was what the Catholic faithful in the Midwest wanted more than anything else. Others have served as chaplains in prisons and jails, as traveling preachers, or as "confessors," priests whose main occupation was the hearing of confessions in larger urban parishes such as St. Peter's Church in Chicago's Loop.

The friars who staffed Quincy University cycled in and out of the college, on their way to and from other kinds of ministry in the Church. This made the college different from a Jesuit institution, where the religious community focuses specifically on education, and where each college is one of a larger population of Jesuit colleges and universities. The Jesuit system functions something like the world of professional baseball, with major league institutions and a farm system for mentoring future leaders. The lack of such a system has been one of the major handicaps in the functioning of Quincy University. Forty years ago, the sociologist David Riesman, describing Catholic and "Negro" colleges, observed that their greatest challenge lay in the recruitment of competent administrators.

The Jesuits are more the exception than the rule in the academic world. Few colleges and universities are part of a larger system, and most began from less than systematic origins. Many important institutions today began as "normal schools," colleges designed to produce teachers for elementary and secondary schools, and evolved into full-fledged universities during the twentieth century. Some of the oldest and most prestigious colleges, such as Harvard and Yale, began as seminaries for clergy.

Quincy College's existence was threatened more than once. A small number of friars with special abilities and devotion to its development kept it going. At the risk of passing over friars whose accomplishments have not come to my attention, and at the risk of offending some people still living, I will highlight several men whose contributions to the College stand out: Frs. Anselm Mueller, Nicholas Leonard, Julian Woods, and Gabriel Brinkman. These men were presidents of the school. Others, like Frs. Pacific Hug, Owen Blum, Tom Brown, Melvin Grunloh, Phil Hoebing, and Francis Jerome Gray, were legendary teachers.

Of the 3,000 friars who have lived in Sacred Heart Province since its beginning in 1858, about 300 are recorded as stationed at Quincy University.

The median number of years that these friars served Quincy University was six years. The mode of their lengths of tenure was two years. The average was ten years, so some of them were here for a long time, some spending most if not all of their careers here.

The total "man-years" of service to the College by Franciscan friars is about 3,000. If those years of service were to be reimbursed in today's dollars, the total contribution would come to about $120 million. As I will explain in more detail later, until the 1970s, the friars did not accept salaries for their services.

"FRIARS"

The word "friar" is derived from the Latin "*frater*," which means "brother." "Minor" refers to Francis of Assisi's preference that his followers remain close to those on the bottom of any social hierarchy in which they might find themselves. A valuing of minority and poverty had enduring and visible effects on Quincy University. The friars operated consistently on shoestring budgets. They were unconcerned about cultivating wealthy donors. They generally avoided management positions. They saw themselves as itinerants, men who could pack up and move anywhere in the world on a moment's notice. For the first fifty years of Quincy College's existence, they assumed that all that was needed to be a teacher at the College was the education required of any priest.

The Franciscan term for this style of operation is "seraphic confusion." The modern term would be "lack of administrative skill." With a few notable exceptions, Quincy College has been led by men who lacked experience in administration. Yet in the midst of this confusion, hundreds, and maybe thousands, of laymen and women (women were first admitted to the College in 1932) say that they received here an outlook on life that they praise and prize.

Trends in higher education in the last twenty years have required more

Figure 1: This chart is based on the names of friars listed in college catalogs from 1871 to 2009. The numbers include lay brothers if they were in the published lists of faculty and staff.

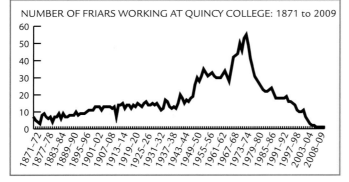

NUMBER OF FRIARS WORKING AT QUINCY COLLEGE: 1871 to 2009

than seraphic muddling. It is appropriate that professional lay administrators now begin to guide the affairs of the University. Francis of Assisi would have approved. He wrote in his "Earlier Rule" (a version of the Rule that was later supplanted by a more official one),

The brothers all, at whatever stations they may be among other people for service and work, are not to be personal attendants, nor secretaries, nor managers in households where they are in service.

"O.F.M."

Before 1897, Franciscans added the initials "O.S.F." (Order of St. Francis) to their names. In 1897, Pope Leo XIII ordered a re-alignment of the many groups of Franciscans that had sprung up over the centuries. The initials "O.F.M." (Order of Friars Minor) became the new identifier.

The Franciscan Order is made up of friars who are ordained priests and friars who are not ordained. Until about thirty years ago, the friars typically described their institutions as operated by "Franciscan Fathers," which suggested that the important work was done by the priests, and that the non-ordained friars ("lay brothers") were performing roles that served the priests in their work. In recent years, the Order throughout the world has made a systematic effort to downplay the differences between ordained and non-ordained. Some have attempted to use the title "Friar" for both priests and lay brothers, but this is not how most men in the history of Quincy University are remembered.

Since this is an historical work, I have chosen to continue to use the term "Father" (abbreviated "Fr.") for priests, and "Brother" ("Br.") for non-ordained friars. To avoid overloading the text with abbreviations, I have chosen to drop the suffix "O.F.M." whenever a name is preceded by "Fr." or "Br." I will specifically identify the occasional non-Franciscan priest who has served at the school when he is referred to.

Until 1921, official Province records did not list the place of residence of lay brothers, friars who were not priests. Therefore, the count of the number of friars at Quincy University during those early years is understated.

Fr. Francis Jerome captures some of the spirit of these men in his description of Br. Novatus Dierken:

... the sharp little hunchbacked man with the phenomenal memory: Br. Novatus Dierken. Franciscan Brothers performed the manual labor involved in operating the college until 1922. The Brothers led a hidden life sequestered from the world and from the Franciscan faculty as well. They only spoke when spoken to; they were not allowed to enter the library-recreation room of the faculty. Their gathering place was in the dining room or at the end of the friary hallway until 1964. Neither newspaper nor radio was permitted for their use. Since Br. Novatus taught mathematics and German to the younger boys, he was allowed a greater degree of association.

COLLEGE OR UNIVERSITY?

Quincy University has had four official names since its founding in 1860. It was known as "St. Francis Solanus College" until 1917, when the name was changed to "Quincy College and Seminary." The words "and Seminary" were dropped in 1970. Then in 1993, the school adopted the name "Quincy University."

I will refer to the institution as "Quincy College" when I am describing events prior to the 1990s, and "Quincy University" after that.

Background and Beginnings
1860 to 1863

THE STORY OF QUINCY UNIVERSITY BEGAN and continues as part of the story of the Franciscan Order, and specifically of the Sacred Heart Province of the Order. In order to set the stage for the history of the University, we need to look at its "pre-history" in the German Franciscan Province of the Holy Cross, and at its roots in a long tradition of Franciscan involvement in intellectual life.

FRANCISCANS AND LEARNING

Francis of Assisi, the founder of the movement and Order that motivated the friars, was a well-off young man who felt called to identify with the "poorest of the poor" (to use a phrase made famous by Teresa of Calcutta). Poverty is in many ways incompatible with learning, and the struggle over the issue has occupied the Order since its earliest days.

Books in the thirteenth century were expensive. Recall that they had to be copied by hand and bound in wood and leather—there were no paperbacks in

PRESIDENTS
Fr. Servatius (Servace) Altmicks,
1860–1862
Fr. Capistran Zwinge, 1862–1863

those days. Even if the labor of copying was cheap (there were lots of monk copiers), the materials had to have been costly. Furthermore, learning requires leisure, and only well-to-do people enjoy such leisure. The rest of the population struggles to survive.

Francis and his first followers did not seek education. It was not long, however, before men who were already learned began to apply to the Order—masters of theology and other sciences at some of the great universities of the age such as Paris and Oxford. Anthony of Padua, the first theology teacher in the Order, came to the Order from the Augustinians. Francis wrote him a letter specifically authorizing him to teach theology. The letter suggests that there were those in the Order who frowned on such activity as incompatible with the poverty that they had vowed.

Alexander of Hales was a master at Paris when he joined the Order in the 1240s. He in turn taught Saint Bonaventure, the scholar who became general minister of the Order and is called its second founder. By the 1260s, there were schools of Franciscan and Dominican friars both at Paris and at Oxford, and the then dominant academic elites tried to get them removed from university life. Both Bonaventure and the Dominican Thomas Aquinas wrote in defense of the mendicant ("begging") Orders as legitimate players in the academic and ecclesiastical worlds.

The Order's history is checkered with schisms and conflicts, periods of growth and periods of decline. Its intellectuals survived the ups and downs, contributing to the story of Franciscan influence on the academic world.

FRANCISCAN DECLINE AND GROWTH

Membership in the Order peaked in the early 1700s, at about 75,000 men. The peak was followed by a drastic decline that nearly wiped

out the Order in parts of Europe. The decline was driven by the spirit of skepticism toward religious belief that came with the Enlightenment. The decline was sometimes sponsored by Christian rulers, for example, the "Sacristan King" Joseph II of Austria, whose ambitious program of secularization involved shrinking religious orders. By 1820, the Order in Germany was a tiny remnant. The Prussian government had forbidden the friars to admit new members, and buildings designed to house hundreds were occupied by handfuls of men.

Ever since the earliest days of the Franciscan Order, there were schisms and reforms dividing it: Conventuals, Observants, Capuchins, Recollects, Alcantarines, Reformati, and Discalceati are the names of some of the split-off groups. The friars in the part of Germany then called "Saxony" were Recollects, and one of the provinces there was called Holy Cross Province.

In the 1840s, the Prussian government of Saxony slightly relaxed its restrictions on entrants to the Order and a revival began, facilitated by a movement to live a more rigorous Franciscan life. The newness of the revival can be inferred from the

« Although drawn in the 1880s, this sketch, probably made from a hot air or helium balloon, shows the terrain of Alstyne's Prairie. One can see, from left to right: the parish school, the parish church, the friary (set back), the 1871 building (present east wing), and the orphanage.

This old photo shows Fr. Gregory, seated in the front middle and surrounded by other friars. The handwritten notations at the bottom of the picture suggest that the group is the faculty of a seminary.

age of the "provincial minister" (province leader) of Holy Cross Province elected in the 1850s, Fr. Gregory Janknecht, who was only twenty-six years of age when he assumed the highest office of his province. It was Fr. Gregory who allowed friars from his tiny German group to leave the mother province and begin a new venture in Illinois. Fr. Gregory continued to lead his province in various ways for the next thirty years. When he died in 1896, he left a German province of 1,000 members and daughter provinces in North and South America, including Sacred Heart Province.

Such growth of course cannot have been the product of one man's leadership—social conditions had to have favored the entry of young men into religious life. People do not become religious solely for spiritual reasons. No doubt the appeal of "coming to America" was one motive for becoming a friar. For young men and women from impoverished peasant backgrounds, becoming a religious and being sent to America was one way to achieve what others were achieving by saving up money for passage across the Atlantic. Some left Germany to avoid conscription into one of the armies constantly warring across Europe. Economic conditions drove many to leave a countryside where a high birth rate and industrialization were making it increasingly difficult to get the necessities of life.

Priests and religious came to America very often at the request of lay people who had migrated earlier and were seeking ministers who could replicate in their new home the rituals and teaching of their earlier lives in Europe. That was true of the men who began Sacred Heart Province.

To sum up the story, the Franciscan Order, just beginning to come back to life in Germany, made the decision to come to America to provide spiritual support for German immigrants in the Midwest. Their two initial settlements were in Illinois. The first was Teutopolis, a small German community four miles east of Effingham in the southeastern part of the state, and Quincy, at that time one of the largest towns in Illinois,

located on the Mississippi River on the western border of the state.

THE CHURCH IN ILLINOIS IN THE 1850s

The Catholic Church in the United States began as a single diocese, with Baltimore as its headquarters (in Church language called a "see"). The state of Illinois then became part of the diocese of Bardstown, Kentucky, then of Vincennes, Indiana, and then of St. Louis. In 1844, the state of Illinois was separated from St. Louis and became a diocese, with Chicago as its see. In 1853, the southern half of the state was split off into a separate diocese. The first location of the new see was to have been Quincy, at that time the second-largest city in the state. However, even before a bishop arrived on the scene, the location of the diocesan see was changed to Alton, a town on the Mississippi closer to St. Louis. The first bishop appointed to the Alton diocese was Henry Juncker, a priest from Cincinnati. He assumed leadership in the diocese in 1857.

Catholics of both German and Irish background had begun settling in Quincy already in the 1830s. The first German parish was St. Boniface, founded in 1839. Shortly thereafter came the Irish parish of St. Lawrence O'Toole, later renamed St. Peter. The church buildings of the two congregations were one block apart: St. Boniface at Seventh and Maine and St. Lawrence at Eighth and Maine.

1860 IN QUINCY

It is worth recalling how fateful a year 1860 was in U.S. history. Just two years before, Abraham Lincoln and Stephen A. Douglas had debated the question of slavery in Washington Square in Quincy, two blocks from St. Boniface Church. Just across the Mississippi River from Quincy lay the slave state of Missouri. Because of the nature of the farmland and the crops grown at the time, slavery was more common in the northern part of Missouri than in the southern, and thus in the area near Quincy. Quincy had its abolitionists, including Richard Eels, a doctor who had been arrested in 1842 for harboring an escaped slave, and whose case was appealed all the way to the U.S. Supreme Court, where it was argued by Stephen Douglas. Douglas had himself lived for a period of time in Quincy.

The Catholic community in Quincy, like the Catholic community throughout the U.S., was not in great sympathy with abolitionism. Pope Gregory XVI issued a decree in 1839 condemning both slavery and the slave trade, but U.S. bishops interpreted the decree as forbidding only the trade, not slavery itself. No American bishop before the Civil War condemned slavery. A tie between Catholic bishops and southern gentry continued past the Civil War, a fact which caused the bishops to drag their feet in efforts to evangelize former slaves. Abolitionism was often promoted by Presbyterians, and Presbyterians in the 1800s tended to be anti-Catholic.

Beyond the cultural attitude of Catholics toward abolitionism there was the German language barrier. The early Quincy College friars lived in a German-speaking world, where issues like slavery were likely to be seen as irrelevant to their interests.

The result of this history is that, in spite of the fateful struggles of the Civil War, emancipation, and reconstruction, there is almost no mention of the issue of slavery or race relations in the early history of Quincy College. The one exception is the case of Augustus Tolton, and his involvement at the College was the result of one courageous and nonconformist friar, Fr. Michael Richardt. The friars at the new college were seemingly oblivious to the national trauma of the Civil War.

At the same time that the friars were beginning a school in Quincy, they were also beginning one in Teutopolis, Illinois, their first home in the Midwest. Throughout the nineteenth century, a rivalry persisted between the Quincy school and the Teutopolis one, St. Joseph's College. At first, the Teutopolis school was built and owned by the bishop of Alton as a seminary that welcomed lay students, and the Quincy school operated as a completely lay institution. Friars came and went between both institutions; many of the faculty and several of the presidents of one school served also in the other. Finally, in 1899, the bishop gave the Teutopolis property to the friars, and they turned it into a seminary exclusively for friar candidates. In turn, Quincy became the place where the bishop educated his college-level seminarians. From 1899 until the 1930s, most priests educated in the Springfield diocese attended Quincy College.

FROM GERMANY TO THE MIDWEST

Here is how Fr. Gregory Janknecht described his vision of what he hoped the friars could accomplish in the Midwest:

> My intention regarding the foundation in America, was, as you well know, apart from helping forsaken souls, to establish a religious community according to the very ideals and spirit of our Father St. Francis. For I was persuaded that under entirely new conditions and after carefully selecting Fathers and Brothers who are animated with true eagerness for their own perfection, many things could be eliminated that exist here [in Germany], which, though not contrary to the Rule, still are not in harmony with a perfect observance of the Rule, nor with ideas of our Holy Founder.

This ideal of "rigor with vigor" continued to inspire friars of the Province for many years, and helped to shape the culture of the College, as will be seen later in this story. The "rigor" is described by Fr. Francis Jerome, quoting Fr. Gregory:

> ... common prayers for about five hours a day, the use of wooden plates, silence in the friary, chime clocks for the church

and dining room, cuspidors for those who chewed tobacco... The friars' day was to begin at four in the morning and close with night prayers at eight in the evening.

The first group of friars to leave Germany, in August of 1858, included two men who were to be involved in Quincy College:

Fr. Capistran Zwinge, age thirty-five. He had been a member of a more rigorous branch of the Franciscan Order, and was especially good at preaching.

Fr. Servace Altmicks, age twenty-nine. He was the only one of the group who spoke English well. He had taught Latin, Greek, and Hebrew to friar students in Germany, and was put in charge of the Quincy school, thus becoming the first president of Quincy College.

A diocesan priest in Germany and pastor in the village of Niederweniger, Fr. Conrad Herman Schaefermeyer had been recruited by Bishop Juncker to come to his Alton diocese. He traveled to the Midwest with the first friars, and was appointed by the bishop as pastor of St. Boniface Church in Quincy, then the largest parish in the diocese.

Fr. Schaefermeyer was single-handedly responsible for several of the most important Catholic institutions in Quincy. In Fr. Francis Jerome's words:

In 1859, he brought the School Sisters of Notre Dame from Milwaukee to take charge of the girls in the parish school. Two years later, he pressured them into purchasing the unused bishop's mansion as a boarding and day school for girls. A cholera epidemic in 1848 had led to the organization of the "St. Aloysius Orphan Society of St. Boniface Parish."

Fr. Schaefermeyer had the Society construct a substantial orphanage at Twentieth and Vine streets. True to the motto "borrow brings sorrow," he did not allow the orphanage to open until it had been paid for—in 1865; meanwhile, the orphans were placed in foster homes. He organized two suburban parishes for his German farmers—St. Anthony in 1859 and St. Joseph in 1867. In 1866, he brought the Sisters of the Poor of St. Francis from Cincinnati to establish St. Mary Hospital.

Fr. Schaefermeyer was also an important figure in the history of Quincy College. Not only did he help to recruit the first friars to staff the school, but he also had an active role in providing for the physical needs of the school in its early years. Finally, he joined the Franciscan Order himself and took the name of Fr. Liborius. He served at Quincy for a while, but then spent most of the rest of his priestly life in places far from Quincy. He is buried in St. Boniface Cemetery in Quincy.

Fr. Capistran Zwinge had been in Quincy in the summer of 1859, and Fr. Schaefermeyer discussed his idea for a school in the town with the friar. The result was a request to the Provincial minister in Germany to authorize a school, along with more friars to staff it. The Provincial chapter in Wiedenbruck in September 1859 granted the request.

In the fall of 1859, Fr. Servace and Br. Honorius Dopp came to Quincy to lay the groundwork for the new school. They rented a building on the southeast corner of Eighth and Maine streets, across the street from St. Peter's Church. They planned to use the first floor for classrooms, the second floor as their friary, and the third floor as a chapel (for the use of the friars—no students would board at the College for several more years).

In February 1860, they were joined by three men who had come to the Midwest that fall:

The parish school, which stood where the west wing of Francis Hall now stands, housed the College from 1865 to 1871.

« This building, on the southeast corner of Eighth and Maine streets, was the first home of Quincy College.

Above: The original St. Francis Solanus Church stood about where the tower of Francis Hall now stands. Fr. Francis Jerome says that architectural design flaws required that iron rods be used to keep the walls from collapsing outward.

Fr. Herbert Hoffman and two seminarians. Fr. Francis Jerome says that the College began classes for fifty students on February 6, 1860, though other sources place the opening date in March of that year. The friars charged no tuition—Fr. Schaefermeyer covered any expenses that arose.

Christian Borstadt, a cabinet-maker and merchant in Quincy, donated four acres of land for the purpose of establishing a parish and school east of the city of Quincy, on land known then as "Alstyne's Prairie." Bishop Juncker wanted a school where his seminarians could receive part of their education for the priesthood, though the school was to be open also to laymen. (The Teutopolis school was not yet in the picture.) The parish trustees formed a building committee and authorized the building of a church, a friary, and a school on the new site, which was separated from the rest of the city by six blocks of empty land.

The new parish and school were named for St. Francis Solanus, a sixteenth-century Spanish friar who had spent much of his life ministering to the native populations of Latin America, especially Peru. Like the Jesuit priests memorialized in the 1988 movie *The Mission*, he used music as a way of appealing to his new flock. Thus, he is often portrayed with a violin. He is also portrayed baptizing an "Indian"—statues above the front entrance to Francis Hall and above the high altar in St. Francis Solanus Church across Eighteenth Street show him in that role. I speculate that the friars chose him as a patron because they saw their new mission as located on the frontier of America, where uncivilized Indians needed evangelization.

Fr. Servace made the mistake of delivering a sermon in St. Boniface Church one Sunday in 1861, calling down a curse on parishioners for their dissension. The upshot was that he left town to begin a parish in St. Louis, and Fr. Capistran Zwinge, a fire-and-brimstone preacher of parish missions, took over the leadership of the school. Fr. Francis Jerome says that Fr. Capistran was hardly the man to inspire confidence in ill-prepared students. He led the enterprise for only a few months. At the end of that time, he turned the enterprise over to the man who was to guide it for over thirty years, Fr. Anselm Mueller.

« This statue of St. Francis Solanus, above the main entrance, honors the sixteenth-century Peruvian missionary after whom the College was originally named.

The Junior College Years
1863 to 1930

GERMAN EDUCATION IN THE MID-NINETEENTH CENTURY followed what was called a Gymnasium (pronounced "Gim-NAH-zee-um") plan. The program was the equivalent of four years of high school and two years of college. The Province maintained this model both in Quincy and in the seminaries in which it educated candidates for the Order.

In 1862, a twenty-four-year-old German friar, not yet ordained to the priesthood, arrived in America; Anselm Mueller. He taught for a few months in the Teutopolis college and was ordained in December 1862. Six months later, he arrived in Quincy and assumed the position of "rector" (president) of St. Francis Solanus College.

In Quincy, the College had no building and hardly any faculty. Fr. Francis Jerome says that when Fr. Anselm took over as rector in 1863, he faced eighteen boys in a room in St. Aloysius Orphanage.

PRESIDENTS

Fr. Anselm Mueller, 1863–1893
Fr. Nicholas Leonard, 1893–1901
Fr. Anselm Mueller, 1902–1909
Fr. Samuel Macke, 1909–1910
Fr. Fortunatus Hausser, 1910–1916
Fr. Gabriel Lucan, 1916–1921
Fr. Ferdinand Gruen, 1921–1927
Fr. Alois Fromm, 1927–1930

One of Fr. Anselm's first achievements was to arrange financing for the construction of a separate college building. It took him several years to finish the project, but by 1871, the College had its own facility. Fr. Anselm continued to manage the enterprise until 1893. He then left its administration to his younger confrere, Fr. Nicholas Leonard. Fr. Anselm returned as president in 1902 and led the College for another seven years after an unfortunate accident crippled Fr. Nicholas.

Fr. Francis Jerome says that the students gave Fr. Anselm the name "the Little General," and he claims that Fr. Anselm jailed students in a space under a staircase next to his office. I wondered if this was just an imaginary embellishment until I found, in a citation from *Landrum's Quincy*, Volume 3, the term "detention room" describing a space on the third floor of the 1871 building. Then again, perhaps Carl Landrum got his information from Fr. Francis Jerome!

COLLEGE REGULATIONS

The catalog of 1874–1875 notes:

The students are always under the vigilant care of their professors and tutors, and form but one family with them. In sickness they are nursed and watched over with parental solicitude, and all the care that parents can desire is given to the wardrobe, dormitories, and all those departments on which health, comfort, and economy depend.

Fifteen "Rules to be observed by the pupils boarding at the College" are listed. Some of the more interesting ones are:

3. Saturday is recreation day, on which the students take a walk in common.

5. No student will be permitted to go beyond the gates of the College grounds or to visit any private house or families without first having obtained permission, which will be granted only for urgent reasons.

7. All use of intoxicating liquors, tobacco, fire-arms, and other dangerous weapons is strictly forbidden.

8. All letters leaving the College or directed to it must pass through the hands of the Rev. Father Rector, and will be subject to be opened.

The 1908–1909 catalog contains the following more emphatic rule:

6. *Cigarette fiends will not be admitted.* [emphasis in the original]

At first the students were almost all from Quincy. Soon, however, the number of students drawn from elsewhere became the dominant element of the enrollment (see Figure 2). This suggests that the College had become attractive to a much wider audience than the original planners had envisioned when they opened a college for local boys.

« This view, taken from southwest of the 1884 parish church (the present parish church), shows the 1894 and 1871 wings before the center 1898 section was built. The building in the foreground, between the church and the College buildings, is the parish grade school.

Bottom: This picture was probably taken soon after the orphanage opened in 1865. The orphanage was on the present athletic field, near the corner of Twentieth and College.

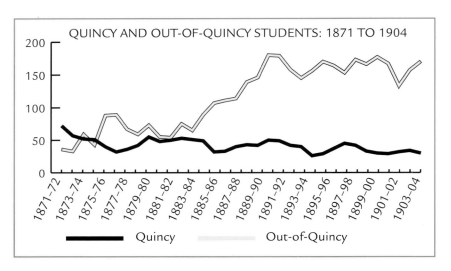

QUINCY AND OUT-OF-QUINCY STUDENTS: 1871 TO 1904

Figure 2: This chart is based on Fr. August Reyling's list of students attending the College. Because he recorded the hometown of each student, it was possible to separate Quincy from out-of-Quincy students.

— Quincy ▪▪▪ Out-of-Quincy

CURRICULA

The 1874–1875 catalog of the College lists the College's curricula. There were three departments: Preparatory, Commercial, and Collegiate. The Commercial department had three levels: First Grammar, Composition, and Rhetoric. The Classical department had six levels: Grammar, Nepos, Caesar, Cicero, Fifth Latin, and Graduates.

All levels in all departments, including the Preparatory all the way to Graduates, took the following courses: Christian Doctrine, English, German, Arithmetic/Mathematics, and History. The upper two Commercial classes took Book-keeping, Drawing, and optional French—these were what distinguished "Commercial" as commercial!

The lower Collegiate levels took Geography and Penmanship, in addition to the five courses common to all levels. All six Collegiate levels took Latin, the upper four took Greek, the upper three took French, and the "Graduate" class took Hebrew.

GRADUATES

Some early catalogs list graduates.

1872-1873 — 3 bachelor of arts degrees
1874-1875 — 2 bachelor, 3 master degrees
1876-1877 — 3 bachelor, 2 master degrees
1877-1878 — 2 bachelor degrees
1878-1879 — 4 bachelor, 2 master degrees
1881-1882 — 2 bachelor, 2 master degrees
1882-1883 — 1 bachelor degree, 7 diplomas in Commercial department
1883-1884 — 4 bachelor degrees, 5 Commercial diplomas

In 1885, the College printed a booklet honoring its twenty-five years of existence as a college. This booklet lists all of the degree and diploma recipients over the twenty-five-year period: nineteen bachelor's degrees, seventeen master's degrees, and twelve Commercial diplomas. Considering that the same booklet lists the names of 906 students who attended the College during that same twenty-five-year period, it is apparent that only a small number of students (5 percent) completed an entire program.

FR. NICHOLAS LEONARD

In 1893, the long administration of Fr. Anselm came to an end—temporarily, as it turned out. His assistant, Fr. Nicholas Leonard, took

The 1893 study hall/auditorium wing of Francis Hall won no architectural awards for elegance—or for that matter, structural stability—but it served several purposes until its demolition in 1983.

This 1910 photo shows the area where students were to spend several hours a day on task.

over and immediately began taking the school in a new direction, a direction which took the form of adding to the college building, creating what we now call Francis Hall. His first construction, in 1893, was a wing attached to the east side of the 1871 building. The new wing housed a study hall on the first floor and an auditorium on the upper level.

The study hall was the room where students spent hours each day in "study periods," blocks of time during which students were expected to be at their desks and on task. My own high school seminary experience, following the same German model, featured a raised platform on which the priest-proctor sat, observing to make sure that students were not reading fiction books or otherwise wasting their time. "Study" meant the study of textbooks and nothing else. There were "writing periods" on Wednesday and Saturday afternoons, during which students could write letters and read other materials.

The auditorium above the study hall seated several hundred people. Plays and musical performances were a regular feature of college life,

and everyone seems to remember that John Philip Sousa and his band played in that room (a bronze plaque by the front entrance of Francis Hall memorializes the event). By the time I arrived at the College in 1970, the auditorium was off limits, on the grounds that engineers had decreed that it was unsafe for large groups of people. The former study hall on the lower level had been converted into a library and classrooms. When Brenner Library was built in 1967, the library half of the ground floor of the older building was turned into a space that came to be known as the "New Old Social Hall." (The "Old Social Hall" was on the southwest corner of the first floor of Francis Hall nearest Eighteenth Street, a space that began as a student dining room and then became the Old Social Hall. In the late 1980s, it was converted into offices for the College president and registrar.)

At some point in its history, the basement of the auditorium wing was excavated to make room for bowling alleys. Finally, in 1983, after a period during which the building deteriorated, it was demolished.

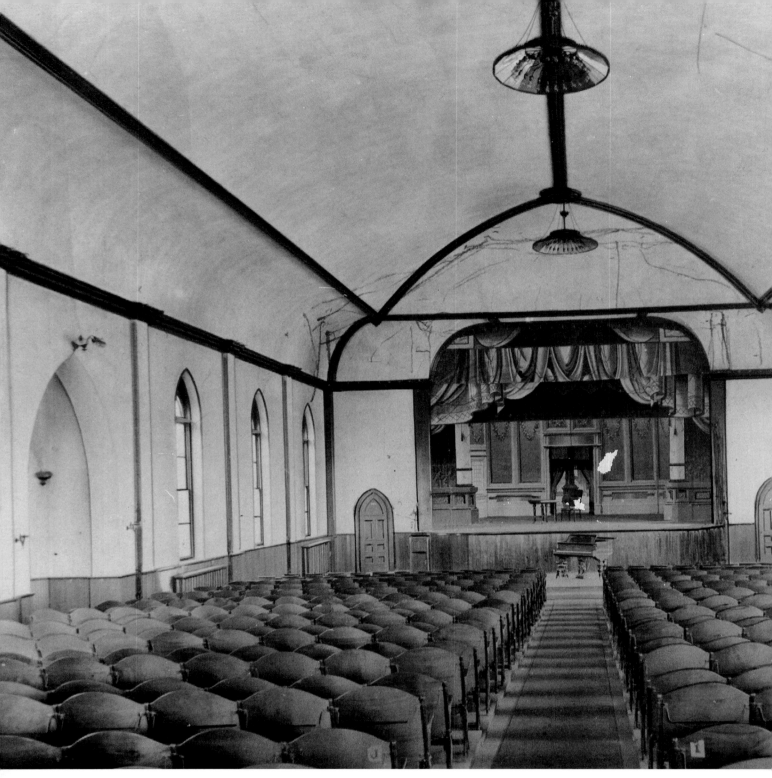

John Philip Sousa performed in this space, which was demolished in 1983 after sitting unused for years.

In 1894, Fr. Nicholas laid the first stones of the present west wing of Francis Hall. The original friary building stood between the 1894 west wing and the older 1871 wing.

In 1898, Fr. Leonard tore down the old friary and replaced it with the present middle section of the Hall, including the tower, complete with a steeple (removed sometime after 1913). It is worth noting that all this building was planned and supervised by a non-ordained friar, Br. Adrian Wewer, who had also built St. Francis Solanus Church west of the College.

In spite of all of this building, enrollment remained more or less steady throughout Fr. Nicholas's years as rector, all the way to the 1930s (see Figure 3).

« Before Brenner Library opened, the library was on the western half of the first floor of the auditorium/study hall wing. The room was partitioned in the middle and the eastern half became a set of classrooms.

This rare photograph shows the 1871 wing with the old friary building to the left of it. College classes were taught in the friary building from 1865 to 1871. After the College moved to the new building, meals were cooked in the friary and carried over to the student dining room in the College building.

» This room began as a student dining room, became the "Old Social Hall," and has now been subdivided to make the registrar's and president's offices.

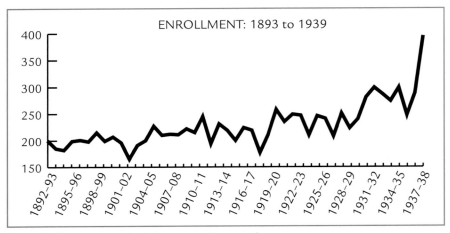

ENROLLMENT: 1893 to 1939

Figure 3: Fr. August Reyling's headcount lists are the basis for the numbers in this chart.

In 1900, Fr. Nicholas was traveling in Omaha when he slipped while getting off a streetcar and fell under the car. His left leg and part of his right foot had to be amputated. He recovered enough to return to the College with an artificial leg, but soon resigned and died of a stroke in St. Louis at the age of fifty-nine.

Fr. Francis Jerome suggests that the death of Fr. Nicholas retarded the progress of the College from the Gymnasium toward a more American model. When Fr. Anselm returned as rector in 1902, the innovation that had characterized Fr. Nicholas's tenure ended.

Br. Pamphilus Schmitz and his crew pose for a picture while building the College chapel in 1911. Two of the workers are African American.

FR. FORTUNATUS HAUSSER

Fr. Fortunatus Hausser took over as rector in 1910 and began plans to build a chapel. His hopes for alumni contributions to finance the project were in vain, but the building went ahead anyway, giving the College the beautiful chapel that still functions as the spiritual center of the University. The architect and project manager for the chapel building was another non-ordained friar, Br. Anselm Wolff. This talented man, who

Notice the fence inside the wall on the lower left, which created a private area for the friars. The tower still has its steeple, which indicates that the picture was taken before about 1912, when the steeple was removed.

This is the original decoration of the chapel. Note the elaborate side altars, the communion rail in front, and the radiators behind the last pew.

» The windows in the 1911 chapel were designed, like thousands of others all over the Midwest, by the Emil Frei Company of St. Louis.

had just finished building the magnificent St. Anthony Church in south St. Louis, had his career cut short by illness before the chapel was even completed. One notable feature of the chapel is its shortened length. The Gothic model for the building would have specified a church one bay longer than the present chapel. The decision to shorten it was made in order to preserve a ball diamond north of the building, between it and Elm Street.

Throughout these early years, as many as seven lay faculty served along with the five or ten friars who staffed the school. One of the best-remembered lay teachers was Charles Percy ("Perk") MacHugh, an English professor who began teaching at the College in 1904 and was on the faculty until 1935.

Professor MacHugh had an interesting past. He was born in Calcutta, India, and received his master's degree at Oxford, where he was a roommate of Rudyard Kipling. He came to Quincy College in 1904 and lived at 1609 Elm until his wife died, whereupon he moved into Francis Hall and lived there until his death in 1935.

Charles Percy ("Perk") MacHugh was a key figure both in academics and in athletics in the early decades of the twentieth century. He poses here with the 1908 team.

A 1921 catalog lists him as teaching English Literature, Oratory, Dramatics, and French. His picture appears in group shots of athletic teams, apparently as an advisor or coach.

MacHugh began a tradition of putting on one of Shakespeare's plays each year, and the tradition was continued through others, most notably Fr. Lucien Trouy. When the space under the chapel was transformed into a theater in 1965, the new space was named after MacHugh, though spelled McHugh. The coincidence that the professor of theater at that time was named Hugh Fitzgerald gave rise to a misconception that the theater was named after Fitzgerald rather than MacHugh.

MacHugh began the first student publication, *The Solanian*, which circulated between 1905 and 1924. The journal functioned more as an outlet for creative writing than as a news source. It was not until 1929 that the present student newspaper, the *Falcon*, began its career.

By 1900, the number of friars on the faculty had risen to a dozen and continued to rise slowly to a level of fifteen or sixteen through the 1920s.

The size of the lay faculty during the 1920s almost equaled that of the friars—the 1923–1924 catalog lists sixteen friars and fourteen lay faculty.

The years of the First World War passed without much effect on the College, except that the words "and Seminary" were added to its name in 1917 in order to protect seminarians enrolled there from the military draft.

The lay faculty are, from left to right: C. P. MacHugh, William Timpe, and Alphonse Birkmeier. Fr. Anselm Mueller, the "Little Giant," is third from the left in the front row. The friar in the middle of the back row is Br. Novatus Dierken, a lay brother who taught German.

"The School for Your Boy" was the school motto during the 1920s.

The year 1930 saw bigger changes begin at the College. Perhaps it was the effect of the Great Depression, or perhaps it was simply the increasing pressure to conform to other American schools, but two events happened which signaled greater changes down the road. In 1932, women were welcomed as students, and pressures from the University of Illinois forced the school to choose between a junior college model with a high school attached, and a four-year college model. The struggle lasted through the 1930s, but finally the college model won out.

ATHLETICS IN THE EARLY YEARS OF THE COLLEGE

Mens sana in corpore sano. "A sound mind in a sound body" was the motto drilled into so many of us when we were young. This led, in our seminary, to a heavy emphasis on sports.

Quincy College was no exception to that approach. Huge scrapbooks in the University archives testify to the fact that 90 percent of the press coverage of the College over the years dealt

A classroom on the second floor (now the WQUB offices) was constructed to look like a bank, so that students in the Commercial program could get hands-on experience. This space later became the College library.

with athletics. While the school was promoting "sound bodies," the town of Quincy was taking an interest in the success of the school's teams—it was part of local pride, part of the story of Quincy as the place where you want your child to grow up.

Varsity athletics are what get press attention, but there have always been other sports on campus, called in recent years "intra-murals." There are no records of these activities preserved in archives. Games that were once called "pick-up games" became scheduled by student activities offices, creating memories and building those sound bodies.

Fr. Francis Jerome has a lengthy description of the place of athletic activities in chapter six of his work, entitled "Student Life." He says, without giving the time frame for the observation, "It proved impossible to keep that bible of baseball, *The Sporting News*, out of the hands of the students." He says that in the early days, the students played on the open fields west of the campus, Alstyne's Prairie. When the orphanage built its new facility in 1918, the College bought the property on which the old orphanage stood, and the present athletic field (the "A-field") came into being. On that space, and the existing space north of Francis Hall, were a baseball diamond, tennis courts, handball courts, and a semi-enclosed space for the game of ninepins. The basement of the 1871 building contained horizontal and parallel bars, a "horse," trapeze rings, and dumbbells. The friars played volleyball in their enclosed garden between Francis Hall and Eighteenth Street—in their habits. Some friars considered it scandalous to play without the habit.

Before the 1893 auditorium wing was built, a swimming pool occupied that ground. It measured forty by seventy feet with a depth of three to eight feet and featured a small number of booths for dressing purposes. Later, the basement of the auditorium wing was excavated enough to allow bowling alleys to be built into the basement.

Baseball seems to have been the first sport to become a part of college life here, paralleling the history of professional sports in the larger society. However,

« This picture, taken after Cupertine Hall was built in 1922, shows athletic activity in the space north of the Hall. The bleachers set up next to that Hall suggest some kind of spectator sport, probably baseball. (The chapel was deliberately shortened to allow for baseball in this space.)

This view of Solano shows the stone wall and tennis courts before they were removed.

This is the cast of an 1899 performance of *The Deaf Mute*. The performances took place in the auditorium, in the now-demolished easternmost wing of Francis Hall.

a 1936 *Falcon* notes that the Hawks returned to baseball "for the first time in several years," suggesting that there were times when the sport went into hibernation. A 1931 *Falcon* recalled that ten years earlier, in 1921, Mart Heinen had become a member of the "Three I Baseball Association" (presumably the three "I's" are Iowa, Illinois, and Indiana). By 1931, Mart Heinen had returned to Quincy to become one of its legendary coaches.

A 1930 issue of the *Falcon* notes that rugby was abolished that year.

Football also seems to have begun in the early decades of the twentieth century. In 1931, the College played the following schools in football: Shurtleff (Alton, Illinois), Burlington Junior College, Moberly Junior College, Culver Stockton, Kirksville Teachers College (now Truman State), Hannibal LaGrange College, Illinois College, and Missouri Wesleyan (Warrenton, Missouri). However, again, in the fall of 1936, the *Falcon* noted that "a dark cloud of despondency descended over the school because of the absence of the football team."

Fr. Edward ("Big Ed") Mueller was one of the leading backers of athletics in the College during the years that he taught here, 1908 to 1922. Fr. Francis Jerome says:

Football had been played by the collegians in the nineteenth century. At some unknown date the sport was dropped as too rough. When "Big Ed" was vice president in charge of discipline, he reintroduced the game... Just when Fr. Edward was looking for someone [as a coach], Mr. Robert E. "Fighting Bob" Harmon came by to watch the team. Mr. Harmon had achieved national renown as a player at Colorado University and had gone on to coach football at the University of Santa Clara. He had become an attorney and was on his way home to Jacksonville to set up his practice when he met Fr. Edward who made him promise to coach. He did so. He returned to QC during the spring of 1922.

In the fall of 1922, Mr. Harmon's duties were enlarged to include the teaching of business law. He fulfilled both teaching and coaching roles until May 1924, when he resigned to become an umpire for the major leagues.

Harmon's first season as football coach did not go well. Quincy College lost all six games. The scores were: Carthage College 48, Quincy 0; Culver-Stockton 26, Quincy 0; St. Ambrose 46, Quincy 0; Quincy City All Stars 20, Quincy 0; Hedding College 7, Quincy 6; and Macomb Teachers College 14, Quincy 7. (Things began picking up toward the end of the season.)

His second year went better: four wins, three losses.

Coach Harmon's replacement for all sports was Mart Heinen. Fr. Francis Jerome describes Mart Heinen:

Fr. Edward ("Big Ed") Mueller was responsible for introducing several sports to the College. He is pictured here with an early baseball team.

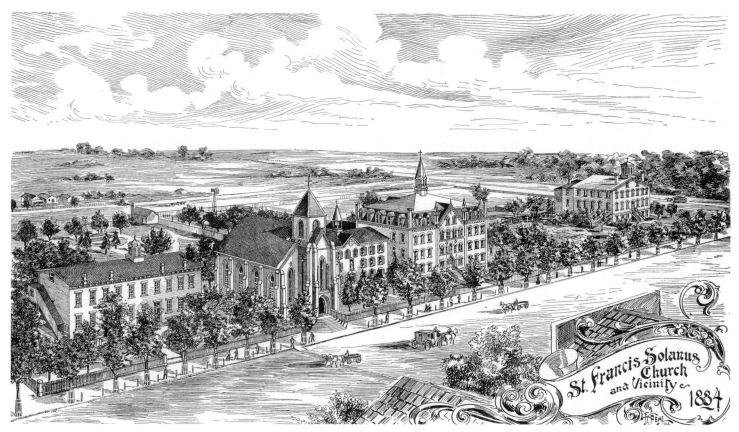

Fr. Ferdinand Gruen had promised the students a revitalized athletic program. Shortly after the opening of school in 1921, "Hap" Harrison resigned as the football coach. A student who had graduated in 1920, Martin Heinen, returned to pinch-hit for his alma mater until a suitable coach could be found. He was to spend the rest of his life at the college. Born in Edwardsville, Illinois, in 1899, he had attended high school at St. Meinrad's, Indiana. He proved to be truly outstanding as a person, student, and athlete... Carl Merkel, his coach during his student days, said of him: "Although only mediocre at the beginning, Mart by his undying determination and perseverance developed into a halfback of the first class. He had speed and courage, and the brains to outwit his opponents." He was elected captain of both the football and basketball teams. He was a member of the only undefeated basketball team in the history of the school. When he left to try out for professional baseball in the minor leagues in the spring of 1921, his fellow students presented him with a silver-plated loving cup. Mart coached the football team only until the arrival of a permanent coach, and then became the assistant coach for the next three years. When Br. Novatus Dierken died in 1921 after twenty-five years of faithful service as the secretary and business manager of the college, Mart Heinen was given that position for a short while. He received no compensation for his services for the first six months he was at his Alma Mater. After that he was paid $780 a year at a time when the average college graduate

This woodcut of College Avenue in 1884 shows, from left to right (west to east): the parish school, the parish church (where the tower now stands), the friary, and the 1871 east wing. The orphanage is the last building to the east. Note the fenced-in area behind the friary.

« This "gymnasium" is now the location of MacHugh Theatre.

in the United States was earning $2,000 a year.

When Bob Harmon was coaching, the team was known as "The Harmonites." After Harmon was replaced by Heinen, the name "Heinemen" was tried but rejected. In 1928, the team became the "Hawks" because the owner of a local sporting goods store, Carl Merkel, had jerseys in stock which were decorated with a hawk. Thus the legendary name of our college teams came into being.

"Big Ed" introduced basketball when he arrived at the College in 1909, and tennis a year later. He was immensely popular with the students, who presented the College with an elaborate framed document of appreciation after his sudden death from pneumonia in 1923. He kept a parrot, which the students taught to say "to hell with Greek." Fr. Emmanuel Behrendt, who lived with him at the time, said that the parrot would stop the horse drawing the milk wagon on Eighteenth Street by calling out the "stop" command. Fr. Francis Jerome says, "After his death, the parrot was loaned to the orphans who lived across the street for a performance of the play *Treasure Island*. In the midst of the performance it began to call 'O Edward.' There was not a dry eye in the audience."

Music has always been an important feature of the Quincy College experience, beginning with the first classes in 1860.

For many years, the original charter hung in the University president's office. It is now preserved in the Brenner Library's archives.

STATE OF ILLINOIS,

Department of State.

GEORGE H. HARLOW, Secretary of State.

« Here, a group of alumni pose with the College tower in the background. The occasion is the golden jubilee of the College in 1910. The friar in car 229 is Fr. Edward ("Big Ed") Mueller.

Fr. Augustus Tolton

AUGUSTUS (OR AUGUSTINE) TOLTON WAS THE FIRST AFRICAN AMERICAN MAN TO BE ORDAINED to the priesthood while publicly recognized as black in this country. Three brothers named Healy, the sons of an Irish man and a slave mother, lived earlier in the 1800s and had remarkable careers (one became the bishop of Portland, Maine, and another became a Jesuit whose name is preserved on a hall at Georgetown University), but because of their father's Irish ancestry, they were able to conceal their African ancestry.

Fr. Augustus Tolton received his priestly education in a seminary for missionaries in Rome. After his ordination in 1886, he returned to Quincy and became the pastor of a black Catholic parish located at Seventh and Jersey streets.

Tolton was born into a slave family in Brush Creek, Missouri, an area near today's Mark Twain Lake. His parents were Catholic slaves owned by a Catholic family named Elliott. When the Civil War began, Tolton's father escaped to St. Louis to join the Union army and was never heard from again. The mother took Tolton and his two siblings and fled to Quincy, where the family found employment in a cigar factory. After the school children at St. Boniface Church rejected Tolton as a student, he was tutored privately by Fr. Peter McGirr, a Springfield diocesan priest who was pastor of St. Peter's Church (then on the southwest corner of Eighth and Maine).

Fr. Michael Richardt, a friar at Quincy College, had acquired a former Protestant church at Seventh and Jersey, named it "St. Joseph's," and began an outreach to black Catholics. Tolton served as a catechist in the church. He wanted to become a priest but no seminary in this country would accept a black candidate. He continued his studies with Fr. McGirr and Fr. Michael and studied at Quincy College, where he is listed as a student in 1878–1879. It was through Fr. Michael's efforts that Tolton was accepted into a missionary seminary in Rome. He was ordained in Rome in 1886.

Tolton was ordered by his superiors in Rome to return to Quincy. He served as pastor in St. Joseph's Church, where he had acted as a catechist years earlier. The pastor of St. Boniface made his life difficult, partly because Tolton was drawing white congregants to his church

Fr. Tolton did catechetical work with children in this church, and then became its pastor when he returned to Quincy after his ordination in 1886. The church was called St. Joseph, and was located on the southwest corner of Seventh and Jersey streets.

who wanted to hear his preaching. He received permission to move to Chicago, where, in the process of forming a parish for black Catholics there, he died prematurely in 1897. He had asked to be buried in Quincy. Tolton's body was returned and buried in St. Peter's Cemetery on Broadway, in the priests' plot.

A Franciscan sister from Dubuque, Iowa, Sr. Carolyn Hemaseth, O.S.F., published a biography of Fr. Tolton in 1974, *From Slave to Priest*. The book was originally published by the Franciscan Herald Press. It was reissued in 2006 by the Ignatius Press, with a new foreword by Deacon Harold Burke-Sivers. A great-great-great-granddaughter of Tolton's sister, Sabrina A. Penn, published a biography of Fr. Tolton in 2007, entitled *A Place for My Children: Father Augustus Tolton, America's First*

Known Black Catholic Priest and His Ancestry. The publisher is listed as PennInk, Chicago, Illinois.

Two historical markers in downtown Quincy note Fr. Tolton's life and work. One is on the corner of Seventh and Maine streets, the location of St. Boniface Church, where Fr. Tolton celebrated his first Mass in Quincy. The other is a block to the south, on Jersey Street just west of Seventh Street, the site of St. Joseph's Church, where Fr. Tolton worked. The church of his childhood is preserved at Brush Creek, Missouri, southeast of Monroe City. Recent work in the cemetery behind the church building presents evidence of slave burials there. No monuments had marked the locations of the graves of slaves there.

From Junior College to Four-year College
1930 to 1946

THE STATE OF ILLINOIS HAD GRANTED A "CHARTER" TO THE SCHOOL in 1873, permitting it to issue degrees (which at that time included even master's degrees). There were no accrediting agencies to monitor the quality of education in colleges.

In June 1930, the College was authorized by the University of Illinois to award a two-year college degree. A few years later, the University extended its blessing from two years to the full four-year college curriculum. Along with the latter blessing came the recommendation that the institution decide whether it wished to continue as a high school or as a college. The struggle to reach that decision continued throughout the 1930s.

The first woman admitted to the College was a religious sister in 1922. Only ten years later, in 1932, admission was opened to all women, lay and religious, and at the same time a series of changes in the legal status of the college began. The movement toward more accreditation seems to have begun under

PRESIDENTS
Fr. Vincent Fochtman, 1930–1936
Fr. John Baptist Koebele, 1936–1942
Fr. Seraphin Tibesar, 1942–1948

Fr. Alois Fromm, president from 1927 to 1930. The admission of women students must be credited to Fr. Vincent Fochtman, who followed Fr. Alois and was president from 1930 to 1936.

THE GREAT DEPRESSION

The 1930s were the years of the Great Depression. Fr. Francis Jerome describes Fr. Vincent's way of coping with the situation:

The monotonous and poor fare served in the boarders' dining room at the west end of the first floor became a legend. Fr. Vincent bought whatever was on sale or in season, e.g., apples served three times a day every conceivable way. A case of rotten eggs and sacks of wormy flour were long remembered. One young man became so tired of baloney all the time that he tacked a slice to the president's door. No tradesman would leave his product without cash payment. There was no fuel to heat the chapel in winter. A glass partition was installed to separate the last three pews from the nave. Here were two radiators. Here the community did their praying. Mass was said out in the cold. The water in the cruets turned into ice before the liturgy was completed. Fr. Vincent paid $75 for a truck—and he would accept almost anything in lieu of tuition, e.g., coal, produce, or labor from students.

Fr. Alois Fromm was the first friar on the faculty to have a doctoral degree. Fr. Vincent became the second. The movement toward greater professionalism continued, and received unexpected emphasis when World War II broke out and the Province sent several friars away for higher studies because the reduced enrollment at the College made their services there unnecessary. Three friars went to Catholic University: Frs. Brian Kirn, Owen Blum, and Brendan Wolf. Three more went to the University of Chicago: Frs. Neal Kaveny, Pius Barth, and Dunstan Velesz. Fr. Victor Herman went to Harvard and Fr. Robert Brinker went to Washington University.

THE ACADEMY

In 1929, the College catalog began to list separate faculties and programs of study for the Academy, for the College, and for the music program. (Music had been an important part of the curriculum from the earliest days of the College.) Fr. Vincent physically separated the high school part of the College from the rest of the school, locating the high school in the auditorium wing in the east section of Francis Hall. The high school had come to be known as "the Academy."

An examination of the relative numbers of students in each program shows that enrollment fluctuated through the 1930s. In terms of

« Fr. Erhard Kuester coaches a student in how to fly a war surplus plane that never leaves the ground. The friars' first cars were war surplus cars, garaged in the small stone building on Eighteenth Street just west of Francis Hall.

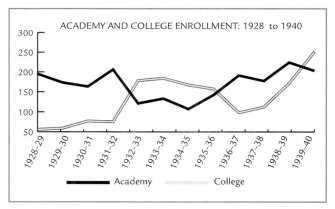

Figure 4: This chart is based on College catalogs from the period. The catalogs recorded high school and College students separately.

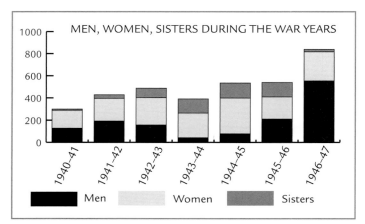

MEN, WOMEN, SISTERS DURING THE WAR YEARS

Men · Women · Sisters

» Figure 5: Because Fr. August recorded Catholic sisters with the title "Sister" before their name, it was possible to distinguish them in the list. A Springfield, Illinois address almost always meant a hospital sister from the Springfield order.

graduates, however, the College program was clearly smaller. There were far fewer college graduates than high school graduates; in some years, fewer than ten students are recorded as graduates of the College.

In 1939, the provincial minister, Fr. Vincent Schrempp, decided that the College section of the school should close, leaving only the Academy. The College president, Fr. John Koebele, mounted a furious lobbying campaign to get the decision reversed. Fr. Francis Jerome says that he organized a secret meeting of the faculty in the College library with paper pasted on the door to prevent any news leaks. He successfully argued that the college was more viable financially than the high school. The decision angered the Provincial Fr. Vincent, the local Quincy population, and the bishop of Springfield, who pulled his seminarians out of the College. The School Sisters of Notre Dame, who had been conducting "St. Mary's Academy" (later renamed "Notre Dame") at Eighth and Vermont streets, agreed to accept boys in their school—they had rejected Fr. Vincent's request in 1934 to do that—but they expected the local pastors to help remodel their school and add a gymnasium. Notre Dame continued as a co-ed school until 1959, when the parishes built a new high school for boys on Jackson Street on the south side of Quincy, staffed by the Christian Brothers. Eventually the Notre Dame sisters vacated the Eighth and Vermont site, assumed management of the Jackson Street building,

made the school co-ed, and renamed it "Quincy Notre Dame."

The back page of the Quincy College catalog for many years featured ads for "St. Mary's Academy, accredited to State University, one of the Strongest, Most Progressive Schools in the Middle West."

THE WAR YEARS

No sooner had the Academy program been discontinued than World War II started, immediately placing every male student in line for either voluntary or involuntary recruitment into the armed forces. Male enrollment dropped. A 1942 *Falcon* article described *Much Ado About Nothing* as being performed by an all-female cast. Total enrollment was saved by programs to train naval cadets and army reservists for the war effort, and by an increasing number of religious sisters, especially hospital sisters of the Third Order of St. Francis from Springfield, Illinois.

The Springfield sisters and Franciscan seminarians during the 1950s and early 1960s never saw the city of Quincy. The sisters were educated at a nursing school at St. John's Hospital in Springfield. Thus Quincy College had more than one campus for the first time. Large numbers of sisters also took summer courses on the campus during those years. All of these women are included in Fr. August Reyling's headcounts. The Springfield nursing school, and a similar one at St. Mary's Hospital in Quincy, received the services of friar teachers, most likely in the role of teachers of religion and ethics.

Fr. Erhard Kuester, a German immigrant with mechanical skills (his brother founded the Kuester Tool and Die Company in Quincy), helped to train the cadets and reservists, who lived in Stillwell Hall, which had been donated to the College in 1941. Fr. Erhard collected war surplus materials, including everything from machine tools to an airplane, and, shortly after the war, began a program in engineering, building the Brower Engineering Building specifically for that purpose on the site of today's Friars' Hall. The airplane did not actually fly, but sat in the backyard of the school, allowing students to examine it and practice on its controls. Older friars, including Fr. Francis Jerome, always credited Fr. Erhard with saving the school.

During World War II, intercollegiate athletics were discouraged in order to save fuel for the war effort.

THE BABY BOOM

The war's end in 1945 freed up millions of men and women, and the so-called G.I. Bill gave them the financial means to attend college, something most of them could not have dreamed of without such aid. Thus began the explosion in enrollment which paralleled the baby boom in demographics in the country. At the same time that returning veterans were raising the birth rate, they were swelling the enrollment at the country's colleges and universities, and Quincy was a beneficiary of that movement.

From 1942 to 1952 the College was presided over by two natives of Quincy, classmates in their seminary years, Fr. Seraphin Tibesar and Fr. Henry Freiburg.

Fr. Seraphin, president from 1942 to 1948, was the son of a former lay faculty member at the College, Nicholas Tibesar. Fr. Seraphin's younger brother, Fr. Antonine Tibesar, devoted his entire life to scholarly research at the Academy of American Franciscan History in Bethesda, Maryland. Another brother, Fr. Leopold Tibesar, was a missionary in Asia, whose correspondence, now preserved in the Brenner Library archives, is a valuable witness to conditions in Japan during World War II, where he spent some years as a prisoner.

In 1946, Fr. Seraphin recruited Fr. Henry on a temporary basis to lead a capital fund drive.

The purpose of the drive was to collect funds for a gymnasium—the College had no gym of its own, and its athletes used the Catholic Youth Organization (CYO) gym at Seventh and Broadway for their games. The space under the chapel, originally intended as a gym, had become a carpenter shop.

The drive was moderately successful, and ultimately enough funds were raised to build the gymnasium in 1950.

The first response to the enrollment increase after the war consisted of the opening of new buildings. The College purchased several small war surplus buildings and located them on the site of the present Centennial Hall. Two mansions on Maine Street became dormitories for women students. "Stillwell Hall," now the Quincy

Fr. Seraphin Tibesar, QC president from 1942 to 1948, was not averse to demonstrating his desire for "a sound mind in a sound body" through athletics. After his service to the College as president and teacher, he became chaplain to St. Mary's Hospital in Quincy.

Stillwell Hall, given to the College in 1941, was a residence for women students until the on-campus residence halls were built in the 1960s. Alumnae describe the majesty of descending the magnificent carved stairway to meet their guests in the living room.

When the male student population exploded after the Second World War, the College acquired a set of used army barracks and set them up at Twentieth and Chestnut, on the site of Centennial Hall.

Museum at the corner of Sixteenth and Maine, was one—it had been given to the College in 1941. The other, at 1651 Maine Street, "Bonfoey Hall," was purchased by the College, and is now a private residence. In 1946, the St. Aloysius Orphan Society was persuaded to sell their orphanage to the College as a dormitory for male students. This building, demolished in the summer of 2008, was renamed Solano Hall. The College relocated two large buildings from munitions factories at Illiopolis, Illinois. One of these buildings, just north of Francis Hall, was opened as a cafeteria, then as a bookstore, and now houses the Hawks' Hangout, a snack lounge for students and staff, as well as the ceramics kilns. A second building, east of the first, housed the chemistry program, and was demolished in 1984 when the College acquired North Campus and moved the sciences to that campus.

Bonfoey Hall, now a private residence on Maine Street, housed women students in the years before Centennial and Garner were built.

How did the man get into this picture of Stillwell girls raking their lawn?

The war surplus barracks, on the site of Centennial Hall, can be seen at the upper right-hand corner of this late 1940s aerial view. The picture also shows the Hawks' Hangout building, the now-demolished chemistry building east of it, and the Brower Engineering Building, where Friars' Hall now stands.

The Expansion Years
1946 to 1970

ENROLLMENT AT QUINCY COLLEGE INCREASED CONTINUOUSLY through the late 1940s, the '50s, and '60s, up until the early '70s. In the 1960s, the baby boom began its impact on college enrollment, and a college education was a way to postpone the military draft imposed during the Vietnam War. It was with the winding down of that war in the early 1970s that enrollment began again to drop.

By 1948, it was decided that Fr. Henry should become the next Quincy College president, and this change was made. During these years, the College began its first attempts to gain accreditation from the North Central Association of Colleges and Universities, the college accrediting agency for the Midwest. It took three tries, beginning in 1947 and finally succeeding in 1954, before the College achieved that goal. It was also during Fr. Henry's tenure that the Quincy College Foundation, the beginning of the College's endowment, was established in 1948. Fr. Henry and a group of local supporters led by Judge John F. Garner were responsible for this development. Prior to that time, the friars had been reluctant to create an endowment, because they considered such an action contrary to their Franciscan Rule. Fr. Henry was also involved in helping to form the Associated Colleges of Illinois in 1952, which continues to be an annual source of contributions to QU and other private colleges and universities in Illinois.

THE SISTER FORMATION MOVEMENT

Many of the hundreds of groups of Catholic sisters in the U.S. had been organized in the nineteenth century by priests or bishops to respond to needs in a local area. A parish needed someone to teach in its parochial school, the pastor would recruit women to do this, and very soon a new religious congregation had come into being. Since elementary teachers in most American schools before about 1930 were women expected to be celibate, the system did not greatly differ from secular American culture. In fact, Catholic religious women enjoyed advantages not shared by their secular counterparts. They received social support as members of religious communities, and benefited from official church approval for their work.

The ad hoc origins of many of these communities meant that girls were sometimes sent out to teach as soon as they graduated from high school. Beginning in the 1930s and '40s, efforts were made to provide better education for these women. The movement acquired a name, the Sister Formation movement, and gathered momentum into the '50s. Quincy College participated in this movement by organizing summer "vocational institutes" for sisters under the leadership of Fr. Pacific Hug.

A parallel development was occurring among hospital sisters, where nursing schools were

organized in connection with hospitals. Quincy College played a significant role in the nursing schools operated in Springfield, Illinois, at St. John's Hospital, and in Quincy at St. Mary's Hospital. By the late 1940s, the names of hundreds of sisters, mostly from Springfield, appear on the lists of students enrolled here. These students, like the Franciscan friars whose seminary was in Cleveland, Ohio, never saw Quincy, but were listed as official students of Quincy College so that their work could be reflected on College transcripts. Thus Quincy College was midwife to the birth of professionalism in several religious communities of women.

AFRICAN AMERICANS AT QUINCY COLLEGE

As was noted in the story of Fr. Tolton, the Franciscans of Sacred Heart Province have not always been in the forefront of efforts to overcome racial discrimination. But, as the story of Fr. Tolton also illustrates, individual friars, and eventually the whole Province, made efforts

« The "gym annex" (today's Hall of Fame Room) was added to the gym through the generosity of the Mart Heinen Club.

Above: Fr. Pacific Hug's summer "vocational institutes" for sisters were a feature of the College for many years. This one took place in 1947. These events were often the first opportunities these women had to experience a college atmosphere and to network with other religious women.

In 2005, Harry Forrester returned to Quincy to reminisce with the African American athletes he had promoted at QC in the 1950s, including Dick Thompson, shown in the above photo. Edsel Bester is in the background.

Herald Whig commemorated their gathering in a special section of the paper with the title, "Only the Net Was White," describing how the team became the first Quincy College team to reach the NAIA national tournament. The *Whig* article describes their situation:

"Racism, discrimination and segregation followed us around," said [Edsel] Bester, 69, a sophomore forward on the 1954–55 team. "Where to stay during our travels? Where to eat? We were not even welcomed at the movies. We could not use certain restrooms. It was appalling."

Opposing fans constantly yelled at and threatened the players. The "n" word bombarded their every movement. Referees' whistles often sounded an extraordinary number of fouls on the Quincy players.

... "[In my four years] at Quincy College, we didn't play against a total of five black players, because many of America's colleges and universities

to welcome the previously unwelcomed into their lives. In the 1930s, the Province assumed responsibility for African American parishes in Chicago, Memphis, and Louisiana, and by the late 1940s, African American candidates were being admitted to the Province's seminaries.

A member of our staff, Kevin Steinkamp, loaned me a clipping showing members of the 1946 football team on which his father played. The picture shows an African American player. The *Falcon* around that time described a player named Earl "Lefty" Johnson, "Negro speedster and thrower of long passes."

In the early 1950s, Quincy College's basketball coach, Harry Forrester, welcomed African American players to his team, and they along with their white teammates quietly fought discrimination whenever Forrester's team faced it, on or off the court. One story has the whole team walking out of a restaurant that was not going to serve its African American players.

In April 2005, several members of that team, along with Coach Forrester, returned to Quincy to recall their experiences. The *Quincy*

» Four of the African American students recruited by Harry Forrester for his 1954–1955 basketball team relax in Cupertine Hall. Elton Crim is lying on the upper bunk and John Snow and Ed Crenshaw play cards while Ben Bumbry observes.

would not even recruit African American athletes," said Bester.

In the fall of 2008, 10.2 percent of Quincy University's student body was made up of African American students. Another 4.5 percent was listed as "other minority," including Hispanic. The University sees the African American and Latino populations as potentially rich sources of student recruits.

FR. HENRY'S PROBLEMS

After the Second World War, football returned to the campus when the Pioneer Conference was organized, consisting of the "oldest colleges in the state": McKendree, Shurtleff, Eureka, and Quincy, with hopes that Aurora and Principia would join. Quincy withdrew from this in 1949.

During the fall of 1951, several football players violated disciplinary rules by failing to return to campus on time after the homecoming weekend. The dean of men, Fr. Evarist Farnand, an inexperienced disciplinarian only recently appointed to the job, suspended them from playing the next two games, causing the team to lose those games. The football coach, Bron Bacevic, was outraged and resigned. Fr. Henry stood loyally by his dean, taking the heat.

Fr. Henry continued as president until 1952, when he left the College to become a highly successful pastor in several of the Province's largest parishes, including St. Peter's Church in Chicago's Loop.

The football program survived the 1951 blow-up, but was ended by Fr. Julian in 1954.

In the meantime, despite the turmoil, enrollment continued to grow.

FR. JULIAN WOODS

Fr. Henry was replaced in 1952 by Fr. Julian Woods.

Fr. Francis Jerome describes Fr. Julian as gifted but autocratic. During his tenure, enrollment grew and the size of the faculty increased from around twenty to between fifty and sixty. The number of friars went from a steady level of fifteen, which had held true since 1900, to a new level between thirty and forty friars. Friar staffing was helped by a large number of young men who were ordained in the early 1950s. These cohorts of friars were to play a major role in the next half-century of the College's history.

One of the high points of Fr. Julian's career was a banquet he organized at which the comedian Bob Hope presided, along with a Hollywood gossip columnist named Luella Parsons.

The building known as "Augustine Hall," a one-story building that occupied the entire southern half of the block west of Eighteenth Street between Elm and Lind streets, was built and named for the general minister of the Franciscan Order, Fr. Augustine Sepinski, who was visiting the Midwest for a celebration of the Province's 1958 centennial. The building eventually became less and less desirable as housing. An attempt was made to renovate one wing into apartments, but even this change failed and the building stood empty until it was demolished in the 1990s. The same period saw the construction of Centennial Hall, Garner Hall, and Woods Hall, all along Chestnut Street. Government loans at very low rates made most of this building possible.

Woods Hall had no name until the 1990s. Until then, the building had been variously referred to as the "married students' apartments," or the "faculty apartments."

Centennial Hall was built as a women's residence, but in recent years, it has housed women in one wing and men in the other.

In 1963, Fr. Julian was replaced as president by Fr. Gabriel Brinkman, a sociology professor.

Friars' Hall opened in 1964. The building, which now seems to those of us who lived there as far too institutional, was seen by the friars at the time as a great improvement over their earlier living quarters on the second and third floors of Francis Hall. One former student described how she and her fiancé met Fr. Gabriel Brinkman for marriage instruction by pouncing on him as the friars marched, in community, from their dining room (in the area now occupied by the Computer Center) to the chapel.

Construction of Friars' Hall had one unforeseen consequence which in retrospect had a negative effect on the perception of the College as a Franciscan school. Until 1964, the friars prayed together in a space at the back of the College chapel set apart by a raised platform surrounded by a railing. The new friary included a chapel for the friars built onto the east side of the main chapel transept and accessible from their new house by means of an enclosed walkway. This made the friars' prayer life invisible to students. In the 1980s, I was astounded to hear a lay colleague who had taught at the College for twenty years express surprise that the friars prayed together.

FR. GABRIEL'S FIRST TERM

The growth in enrollment continued, and with it, growth in the number of lay faculty and staff. The friars, whose presence had formerly dominated the atmosphere of the College, were soon to become a minority presence on campus. At the same time, the Second Vatican Council in the larger Catholic Church opened the door to changes in the customs of Catholic religious life, producing what the writer Garry Wills characterized at the time in the title of a book as "bare, ruined choirs." The most visible effect of the Council at the College was that the friars, with a few exceptions, began to wear secular clothing, abandoning the brown Franciscan robe (which they call a "habit") which until then

Augustine Hall's front entrances lined Elm Street.

« The "married students' apartments" were built in the early '60s to accommodate older students and some faculty.

Fr. Gabriel established the Administrative Council, consisting of representatives of the major areas of the school, which became the primary policy-making body. He also created the offices of Financial Aid, Placement and Development, Counseling Center, and the director of student activities position.

Quincy College led in innovations which were later to be adopted by many other institutions. One of these innovations was the institution of soccer as a varsity sport, begun in 1964 under John Ortwerth, Roger Francour, and Frank Longo. The St. Louis area had long been a hotbed of soccer interest in the nation, and Quincy College was able to use its geographical proximity to this pool of players to great effect. As a member of the NAIA athletic association, Quincy soon rose to national prominence in soccer. Quincy won a total of eleven NAIA national soccer championships between 1966 and 1981, including five consecutive championships (1977– 1981) under Coach Jack Mackenzie, becoming the first and only men's soccer team from any division (NAIA, NCAA, and NJCAA) to achieve that accomplishment. The team was originally coached by Roger Francour from 1964 to 1968. Mackenzie has led the men's program since then. The men's program was so successful that a women's soccer program was subsequently established in 1983. Led by Coach Bill Postiglione until 2005, the women's program finished in the top twenty in national rankings nine times and advanced to two consecutive semifinals of the Division II national tournament.

Fr. Gabriel Brinkman led the school during two separate six-year terms as president.

they had worn in and out of the classroom. The abandonment was seen as a way of returning to the roots of the Franciscan movement, with the argument that the traditional robe was the garb of ordinary working people in St. Francis's time.

Fr. Gabriel took control of the College with two friar confreres, Fr. Peter Damian Holzer, academic dean, and Fr. Mel Doyle, dean of students. These three continued the program of building begun by Fr. Julian. Padua Hall opened in 1966, Brenner Library in 1967, and Willer Hall and the College Center (cafeteria) in 1970. Enrollment during Fr. Gabriel's first term shot up from a headcount of 805 in 1963–1964 to a headcount of 2,038 in 1970–1971, an increase of more than 100 percent. Total staff size went from fifty-five to 128. There were twenty-eight friars on the faculty in 1963, and fifty-three in 1971. The atmosphere was heady, characterized by success and marred only by the increasing national struggle over the Vietnam War.

Another innovation by Quincy College was to start the academic year in August and end the first semester before Christmas. At the time, the standard practice in both college and lower schools was to begin in September and complete the first semester in January. The change was justified on the grounds that it would give our students a competitive advantage in looking for jobs over the Christmas break and in the spring.

THE MART HEINEN CLUB

In 1947, a group of men organized to provide support for Quincy College's athletic programs, especially football, calling themselves the Quarterback Club. The term "Quarterback" became inappropriate when the College dropped football as a varsity sport in 1954, but the group continued supporting other Quincy College sports, especially basketball. The group renamed itself the Mart Heinen Club, in honor of the legendary coach and staff member described earlier in this book.

The Mart Heinen Club was named in honor of the legendary athletic coach and staff member.

One feature of the Club's history which helped make Quincy the basketball town it is today was the Mart Heinen Holiday Tournament, held each year during the week after Christmas. The tournament, which began in 1954, drew nationally known teams to Quincy until its final year of 1988. It flourished especially during the years when John Ortwerth was athletic director. Ortwerth followed a policy of attracting the most difficult competition he could find to participate in the tournament. The result was that, while Quincy College rarely won its own tournament when Ortwerth was director, the caliber of the play in the tournament added greatly to its prestige and that of the College. His strategy did not keep him from being the all-time "winningest" coach, with a record of 259 wins and 173 losses, a 0.600 percentage. His percentage

was exceeded only by his successor, Sherrill Hanks, who did not win as many games but had a percentage record of 0.668.

Each year, the Club sponsored a "Continental Brunch," the centerpiece of which was the raffling off of a new luxury automobile. Tickets were several hundred dollars each. Each ticket holder was issued a key to the car. Ten of the keys opened the car door, allowing the recipient to select one of ten keys inside the car. Only one key opened the trunk. Br. Clete Van Ackeren, whose portrait adorns the wall of the Hall of Fame Room along with that of Mart Heinen, described to the author the chore of making sure that the key system worked as planned. He had to go to the cafeteria the night before the event and test every key.

In 1962, the club started the Mart Heinen endowed scholarship fund in the Quincy College Foundation, which provides annual earnings to help pay for athletic grants.

The Mart Heinen Club, which first admitted women in 1986, continues today as a dedicated group of individuals and businesses that volunteer their time and resources to help Quincy University athletic teams. The club coordinates several special events to raise funds for the Hawks and Lady Hawks including golf tournaments, a chili cook-off, and holiday basketball tournaments. Some Mart Heinen members also serve as ticket-takers and operate concession areas during QU athletic events. The club helps to sponsor team trips, purchases athletic equipment and supplies, and assists with facility improvements.

COMPUTERS COME TO QC

In the 1960s, the College began its first moves toward computerization. Hollerith cards (the three-by-seven-inch cards that were commonly called "IBM cards") were used to process student registration and financial information. The cards were read in massive machines the size of large desks, and programmed by connecting wires on boards that could be removed for programming and then inserted into the machines. Two friars,

Brs. Clete Van Ackeren and Marvin Schulgen, were in charge of this operation. They were assisted by Fr. Robert Francis Dentzman, a mathematics professor. In 1969, a machine similar to the old ticker-tape machines used by news organizations was connected to a computer at the Illinois Institute of Technology in Chicago. This was followed shortly by a system in which Hollerith cards were read on campus and processed at the University of Iowa in Iowa City. The cards were submitted in the evening, and hopefully by the following day the results could be printed out on campus. If a mistake had been made in programming, the offending card had to be removed from the deck, re-punched, re-inserted, and the deck submitted that night for processing the next day.

A great advance came when programs could be entered on a computer terminal and processed instantly at the University of Iowa. Eventually the College acquired its own processing hardware, and the present system came into being.

MCHUGH THEATRE

In 1965, a professor of theatre, Hugh Fitzgerald, presided over the construction of McHugh Theatre in the space beneath the chapel. "Fitz" watched over the space like a parent, screening everyone who entered and requiring food and drinks to be left outside. His concern for the physical facility was surpassed by his concern for theatre performance by the students. The department regularly scheduled challenging plays.

When the College faced retrenchment in the 1980s, Mr. Fitzgerald discontinued the program as an academic major, arguing that one could not have a credible major with one faculty member. Theatre has continued, however, but on a less formal basis. The recent renovation of McHugh Theatre gives promise that a revival of a full-scale theatre major may become possible.

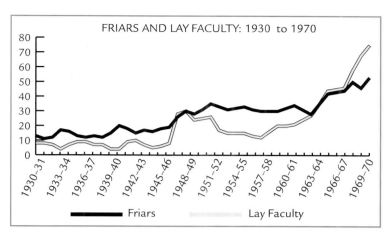

FRIARS AND LAY FACULTY: 1930 to 1970

—— Friars   ········ Lay Faculty

Figure 6: College catalogs for these years are the basis for the numbers behind this chart.

BRENNER LIBRARY

The College library has always occupied locations within existing buildings throughout its early history. The construction of Brenner Library, named in honor of Dr. and Mrs. Frank Brenner for their years of dedication and commitment to the College, in 1967 represented a huge advance in information storage on campus. A human chain was organized to move the books from Francis Hall to the new location, which was accomplished accurately and efficiently. Fr. Jovian Lang handled the transition from the old to the new building, and Fr. Victor Kingery took over the position of head librarian in 1970, a position he held until his retirement in 2000.

One very notable addition to the new building was a special temperature-controlled room, masterminded by Fr. Jovian, which houses a large rare book collection, including many pieces that were part of the library that the Franciscans brought to America from Germany. Today, Brenner Library's rare book collection accommodates over 4,000 volumes of books, fifty-seven of which are some of the oldest and rarest books in print. These esteemed fifty-seven are known as "incunabula" and are registered with the United States Library of Congress.

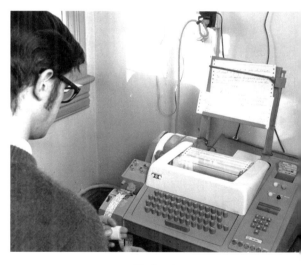

Technology comes to Quincy College. This first 1969 campus "computer" featured a punched paper tape, seen to the left of the machine and wound around the student's finger. The information was sent electronically to Illinois Institute of Technology in Chicago for processing.

Bonfires were a traditional way to celebrate special events, such as Homecoming. This one took place at the 1953 Homecoming weekend.

ʌ While Quincy College has seldom been in the forefront of social protest, its faculty and students have quietly played roles in many important social movements. A more public protest was this 1968 march in favor of peace passing the front of Francis Hall along College Avenue.

« Virgil Niewohner, who has taken tickets at every Hawk game for decades, is still at it in this March 2008 picture.

A 1955 alumna named Toni (Powers) Collins provided this picture of herself talking with Hal McGinnis. Mr. McGinnis went on to become a benefactor and Board member of the College.

Top: McHugh Theatre was constructed in 1965 in the space under the chapel, originally designed to be a gymnasium.

Bottom: Someone staged this dramatic still shot of the cast of a 1968 presentation of Edgar Lee Masters's 1915 play, *Spoon River Anthology*.

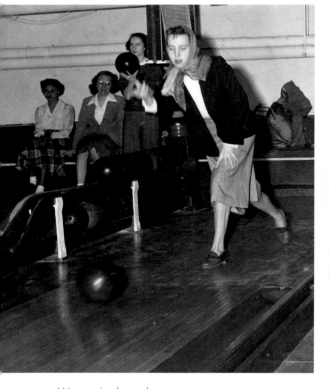

＾ Women in those days dressed more formally for bowling. The alleys were in the basement of the auditorium/study hall wing.

» An arts festival in 1961 was scheduled in the Old Social Hall, the space now occupied by the president's and registrar's offices.

The College's address was 1831 College, because College Avenue ran right in front of Francis Hall. The street was closed in 1966.

« Benny DiDia conducts a 1954 orchestra rehearsal.

This is another view of College Avenue, taken in the winter of 1950 from the front steps of the main entrance of Francis Hall.

Jack MacKenzie soon joined Frank Longo in coaching the new sport of soccer at QC in the 1960s. Here they watch a game together.

Augustine Hall, on Eighteenth and Elm streets, was the first residence hall constructed at Quincy College.

This is how the gymnasium looked before the annex was added.

In 1967, the opening of Brenner Library meant that the College library had to be moved from Francis Hall to the new facility. A human chain was organized to do the job, which was accomplished accurately and efficiently.

Fr. Victor Kingery supervised the library for over thirty years. His quiet demeanor hid his resolute pursuit of technological innovations in library work, especially those involving computers.

The latest thing in the teaching of languages in the 1960s was a "language lab," featuring booths with earphones and a master console from which the teacher could speak to the students.

Every College graduation featured a group picture. This 1960 graduation picture includes extra church dignitaries because 1960 was the centennial year of Quincy College.

The Transition Years
1970 to 1997

FR. TITUS LUDES

Fr. Titus Ludes had been an important figure in the Quincy College education program until 1964, when he took over as principal of Hales Franciscan High School, a newly built school for black students in Chicago's inner-city South Side. However, he returned in 1970 to replace Fr. Gabriel, whose term was coming to an end.

Fr. Titus was president during the successful Partnership Fund Capital Campaign, which exceeded its $3.5-million five-year goal, and continues, over thirty years later, to receive contributions to scholarship funds established then. He was also president when the College bylaws were amended to permit the participation of lay members on the Board of Trustees. This has enabled the University to utilize the expertise of many individuals since then. He also established a Strategic Planning Committee.

PRESIDENTS
Fr. Titus Ludes, 1970–1977
Fr. Gabriel Brinkman, 1977–1983
Fr. James Toal, 1983–1997

Fr. Titus had the misfortune of taking over at the precise moment when the great expansion of the 1960s was coming to an end. Enrollment had peaked in 1970–1971 with a headcount of 2,166. By 1975, it was down to 1,527, a drop not nearly as dramatic as the earlier rise. What turned the situation around, at least temporarily, was the innovative relationship that the College developed with a new local institution, John Wood Community College.

JOHN WOOD COMMUNITY COLLEGE

Early in the 1970s, the state of Illinois mandated that every part of the state had to have access to community college education. Quincy College administrators, led by Fr. John Leonard Ostdiek, decided to be proactive, and took the lead in constructing a model of a community college in which existing colleges would provide instruction to community college students, with the community college itself providing only administrative services. The new institution was to be called "John Wood Community College," named for the founder and early mayor of Quincy, who rose to become governor of the state in 1860. Participating colleges were Quincy College, Culver-Stockton College in Canton, Missouri, Hannibal-LaGrange College in Hannibal, Missouri, Southeastern Iowa Community College in Keokuk, Iowa, Gem City Business College, and Quincy Technical School (now Vatterott College). The community college district paid the participating colleges to teach its students. The arrangement came to be referred to as the "common market," a term used at the time for the movement in Europe that eventually became the European Union. The college began in rented offices in downtown Quincy, moved to a wing of Our Lady of Angels Seminary (now QU's North Campus), and then purchased an elementary

school building that had been built by the Quincy Public School system only a few years before.

Quincy College benefited financially from its instruction of John Wood students, but with the money came some attached strings. Courses taught in community colleges had to be approved by the Illinois Community College Board, which meant that Quincy College had to adapt its curriculum and syllabi to community college standards. John Wood participation in Quincy College sports became an issue. Such participation was approved for men in 1975 and for women in 1977, but was later reversed by the NAIA. John Wood began to develop its own independent athletic programs.

The common market concept had wide public support because it seemed to promise an efficient delivery of quality education. Graduates of John Wood who went on to other four-year colleges were reputed to be better prepared for upper-level college work than students from other community colleges. To preserve confidentiality, the common market agreement specified that the class lists distributed to Quincy College instructors would not reveal who was a John Wood student and who was a Quincy College student. However, the common market system developed problems. The most serious problem was that, in the eyes of Quincy College administrators, John Wood was not carrying the full cost of educating its students, with the result that Quincy College was subsidizing community college education, something it could ill afford to do.

The fall of 1976 saw 276 full-time and part-time students attending Quincy College classes as John Wood students, 18 percent of Quincy College's enrollment that fall. The percentage of John Wood students at Quincy College rose steadily from year to year, until it peaked in 1981–1982, when 922 John Wood students made up 48 percent of the 1,940 students attending Quincy

« The College flagpole is a gift from the Knights of Columbus.

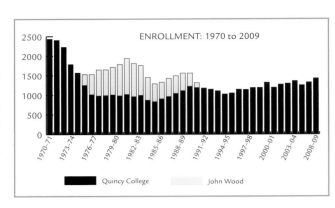

ENROLLMENT: 1970 to 2009

Quincy College John Wood

Figure 7: These figures come from the office of the QU registrar. They are for the fall semester of each year. The registrar's numbers cannot be compared directly with Fr. August's because the registrar can record a student more than once in a year. Fr. August, who ended his record in 1975, recorded each student only once, but included spring, summer, and fall sessions. As a result, his numbers are higher than the registrar's, which report only one semester.

Since then, four program-specific agreements between the two institutions have been signed that build on the institutional level agreement of 2004. These program-specific agreements expedite the transfer process for students wishing to begin their college studies at John Wood and complete them with a bachelor's degree at Quincy University.

ENROLLMENT DECLINE

Staffing at the College had grown in response to an increase in enrollment. Figure 8 shows the enrollment and staffing picture.

Enrollment peaked just over 2,000 in 1970. In response to the growth in enrollment, which began in the early 1960s, the number of lay faculty increased, from twenty-five in 1959 to ninety in 1973. As enrollment dropped by 600 students between 1970 and 1975, the size of the staff dropped only slightly, to about seventy-five lay and thirty friar faculty. The John Wood influx of students pushed up enrollment in the early 1980s, but in 1984, just when the John Wood influx began to decline, faculty size remained near its all-time high.

FR. GABRIEL'S SECOND TERM

Fr. Gabriel Brinkman resumed the presidency of Quincy College in the summer of 1977. The decision to appoint him to a second term was made in an atmosphere of confusion among the friars that may be attributed to a lack of communication.

In contrast to his first term, Fr. Gabriel's second term seemed to lack the momentum and

QU's relationship with John Wood Community College continues to be important. In this more recent photo, administrators of the two schools pose together. Standing, left to right: Larry Fisher, David Schachtsiek, and John Letts, vice presidents at the two schools, and the two seated presidents, Sr. Margaret Feldner and Bill Simpson.

College. After that the percentage and number began to drop (see Figure 7).

The last John Wood students attended Quincy College in the 1991–1992 school year. By that time, only about 10 percent of students on campus were enrolled as John Wood students. In the intervening years, John Wood left its quarters in the former elementary school and began to build its own campus on the southeast side of Quincy.

In 2004, an articulation agreement was signed by the presidents of Quincy University and John Wood Community College which states that JWCC students completing sixty-four credit hours in an associate's degree in arts or science will fulfill QU's freshman and sophomore general education requirements. Additionally, JWCC provides religious studies courses to allow its students to fulfill QU's six-credit-hour theology requirement.

innovation that defined his previous presidency. The team that supported him so successfully in 1963 was gone—two of the most important men, Frs. Peter Damian Holzer and Mel Doyle, had left the College.

Nonetheless, Fr. Gabriel reversed the enrollment decline of Fr. Titus's last two years as president. The student headcount increased from 1,532 the year before he became president to 1,809 his last year, a 27-percent increase. This was during the difficult economic times in the late 1970s and early 1980s that included high inflation, high unemployment, a recession, and a stock market decline. He began discussions on establishing a joint bachelor's degree program in nursing with Blessing Hospital, which was eventually developed in 1998, and the Master in Business Administration (MBA) degree program, which was eventually developed by Fr. Melvin Grunloh, chair of the Business Department in 1984.

BOARD STRUCTURE

Throughout the history of the College, its Board was made up of friars on the faculty, which meant friars living in Quincy. Minutes of the Board through the 1950s and '60s show the same four friars making up the annual meeting of the Board; most business concerned official approval for the government loans needed to construct the new residence halls.

By 1970, during the presidency of Fr. Titus Ludes, the idea of enlarging the Board arose, with the realization that such enlargement would require a more formal arrangement between the

An April snow in 1975 brightened the campus.

friary and the College. The arrangement was gradually worked out, and in 1972, the Board welcomed its first lay members, Ralph Huck and Gertrude Penick. Thomas A. Oakley and Frank Strieby were elected shortly thereafter. At the same time the Board was structured so that Sacred Heart Province would elect two Board members, called the "Provincial members," and the friary would elect two, called the "collegiate members."

It was after Fr. Jim Toal became president that the bylaws were rewritten to exclude the membership of local friars on the Board. That arrangement had created the anomalous situation where a local friar as a Board member hired the president and was at the same time, as a faculty member, subject to the president. Frank Kabbes was elected as the first lay chairperson in 1994.

CONTRIBUTED SERVICES

For the first one hundred years of the College's existence, there was no distinction in finances between the College and Sacred Heart Province. Whatever money was received for work at the College was used to support the friars and to reimburse lay staff for their services. The services of the friars represented a huge financial subsidy to

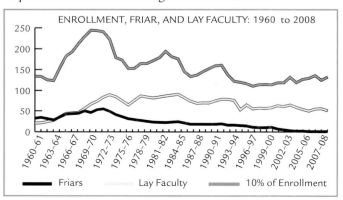

ENROLLMENT, FRIAR, AND LAY FACULTY: 1960 to 2008

Friars — Lay Faculty — 10% of Enrollment

« Figure 8: Enrollment numbers come from Fr. August (up to 1975) and the registrar (after 1975). Numbers of friars and lay faculty are based on the College catalogs. Enrollment numbers from the registrar would be somewhat lower than the ones shown here.

» In the 1970s, registration for classes took place in the gym. Each department staffed a card table. Final exams were also held in the gym, with card tables spaced far enough apart to discourage observing one's neighbor's work. The idea probably came from Harvard University (Fr. Victor Hermann, the academic dean, had studied there).

Top: Ann Bergman taught physical education courses from 1968 to 1998.

Bottom: Dr. Ken Conroy became the first lay academic dean in QC history when he came here in 1975. He retired in 1993 and continued to be active in POLIS, a program offering noncredit courses for seniors.

the College. The saying was that "the friars' services are the endowment of the College." This was true, but the system had the perverse effect of allowing the College to neglect the creation of an independent endowment financed by alumni and other donors. Sporadic efforts to create such an endowment had been made throughout the College's history, but a sustained effort only began in 1948 with the creation of the Quincy College Foundation, which had a board independent of the College (at the time the friars owned the College, and the Franciscan Rule forbade the friars to own property).

As the school became more professionalized, the friars devised a system known as "contributed services." Under this system, each friar was assigned a salary or pay rate based on the prevailing rate for his job description. The finances of the College were gradually separated from the finances of the Province and friary. For each pay period, the friary would receive one check based on the services of all of the Quincy College friars for that period. However, because the school was seen as a ministry of the Franciscan Province, 50 percent of each check was returned to the College. In effect, each friar worked for his prevailing pay rate and donated half of what he earned back to the College.

By the early 1970s, it was becoming apparent that the Province was finding it more difficult to provide friars for the College. In 1971, the year when the largest number of friars chose to leave the Order, the number of entering candidates was also decreasing drastically. The agreement was renegotiated: the Province would return 50 percent of the total friar income to the College if thirty friars were on the staff. If the number of friars dropped below thirty, the Province would return an additional one half of 1 percent of the combined income to the College. Thus, if twenty-nine friars were employed, the Province would return 50.5 percent of the income for the pay period. This was intended to give the Province a financial incentive to maintain staffing for the College.

This system worked for only a few years. As the number of friars in the Province continued to decrease, the agreement was again renegotiated. At one point, the contribution was 30 percent of the total services. Eventually, by the mid-1990s, the contributed services system was dropped entirely.

The friary building, Friars' Hall, was financed by a government loan, which required a yearly $60,000 payment. This payment was taken from the friars' portion of their income. The expectation was that, at the end of the forty-year period of the loan, set to conclude in 2004, the friars would hold the title to the building. In fact, by that time, the building had become unsuitable for friar housing, and the friars built a new friary at Twentieth and Elm streets and accepted the University's ownership of Friars' Hall. The University sold the property on which the new friary was built to the Province for one dollar.

RETRENCHMENT

Fr. James Toal came to Quincy as the new College president in 1983. As a member of the Franciscan Holy Name Province, based in New York, he was the first man from outside the Sacred Heart Province to direct the College. He arrived with a reputation as a competent and decisive administrator.

After large deficits during his first two years, he took the College into the painful process known as "retrenchment," a legal procedure by which the protections of tenure can be voided when an institution needs to reduce staffing in order to survive. A faculty committee was charged with the task of determining who would stay and who would go. The 1983–1985 catalog lists ninety-

two faculty; the next catalog, 1986–1987, lists seventy-four.

In 1985, a former athletic director, basketball coach, and professor of physical education, John Ortwerth, led a successful campaign to get football reinstated as a varsity sport at the College. The argument was that, while the sport would not support itself by gate receipts, it would attract students who would not otherwise attend Quincy

College. Football would also remedy an increasing imbalance of male and female students—female students were beginning to outnumber male students by a sixty/forty ratio. The goals were realized. The gender imbalance was remedied and a projected increase in enrollment of thirty students was exceeded already in the first year when forty students enrolled as part of the program.

At first, football at Quincy College was played as part of Division III of the NCAA, which did not require the school to provide athletic scholarships for the players. In 1995, the NCAA changed its rules and required that an institution had to play all of its varsity sports on the same level. QU had

In this 1989 picture, students fill their plates at a cookout under the ambulatory leading to Friars' Hall.

The most striking feature of Friars' Hall before 2003 was the tile screen which covered all the windows of the building. The screen probably saved energy by deflecting the sun from most of the building during the summer, but it greatly restricted the view of the occupants.

to demote its soccer program from Division I and elevate its football program from Division III.

As the 1980s moved into the 1990s, Quincy College made other changes. The traditional "departments," which by the late 1980s had grown to nineteen, were replaced by six divisions. In 1993, the school name was elevated from Quincy College to Quincy University.

THE FACULTY SENATE

Members of the faculty, concerned that the College was devoting a disproportionate share of its resources to athletic programs, had begun a Faculty Senate in 1979. The Senate struggled

» College cheerleaders were well organized in this 1992 shot.

during the last years of Fr. Gabriel's term. Fr. James arrived with the official policy of working productively with the Senate; however, the relationship between Fr. James and the Senate gradually grew more confrontational.

In the spring of 1997, Fr. James announced his intention to return to the Franciscan Holy Name Province, in New York, effective at the end of the semester.

OTHER DEVELOPMENTS

This book is dedicated to Joe Bonansinga. Among his other contributions to Quincy College, Joe kept alive memories of Fr. Lucien Trouy, who had sponsored Shakespeare productions here during his years on the faculty. In 1996, Joe traveled to Wisconsin to celebrate Fr. Lucien's one-hundredth birthday, and inspired a donor to create the garden space between Francis Hall and Eighteenth Street centered on the statue of St. Francis. Fr. Lucien had used that statue as the centerpiece of a flower garden and pond when he lived in Quincy. The story was that the garden contained every plant mentioned in any of Shakespeare's plays.

CAMPUS MINISTRY

During the middle of the twentieth century, the College began to name one of the friars as "chaplain" to the College. This position, which at first was simply an added responsibility tacked on to the duties of a regular faculty member, became full-time in the early 1970s. The remaining friar-priests on the faculty continued to see themselves as informal chaplains. Fr. James Wheeler, the first full-time chaplain, served from 1973 to 1985. After Fr. James, a succession of full-time sisters, lay brothers, and laymen were hired as campus ministers. Staffing reached its peak in 2008, when

Bob Blazel was a mainstay in the sociology, social work, and criminal justice programs, from his return to campus in 1968 (he had graduated from QC earlier) until his retirement in 2005.

the office included two full-time lay people, one of them hired to minister specifically to non-Catholic students, and one full-time friar-chaplain. The office once again realigned in 2009, giving the friars a more active role and strengthening their presence on campus.

The ministry operated out of various locations: first, a room next to the chapel in the lobby area of Francis Hall, and then a series of houses on Lind Street. One campus minister, Br. Thom Smith, received a grant to renovate the garage area of the Campus Ministry house into a meeting space, which received the name of "Frank 'n Clare's." Campus Ministry operated from Frank 'n Clare's until relocating to the lower level of the Student Center building during the summer of 2009.

In 1996, the old St. Francis garden statue was moved slightly to a garden area newly landscaped and dedicated to the memory of Fr. Lucien Trouy.

» Fr. John Joe Lakers began teaching philosophy at Our Lady of Angels Seminary in the 1960s. Besides playing important roles at QC, he has offered spiritual direction to hundreds of married and about-to-be-married couples.

Over the years, student masses have been celebrated outdoors. Here Fr. Kevin Downey presides at a mass on the lawn just east of Penny Lane.

Fr. Francis Jerome confers with Hugh ("Fitz") Fitzgerald, while a student observes.

College athletics
continued to thrive
during the late 1980s.

« Elvis Turkovich gets ready to pass
in a 1988 game.

» Fr. Tom Brown painted a ceiling-high mural of Assisi on the wall of the dining room in Friars' Hall. He painted Fr. Francis Jerome into the "*Carceri*," (which means "jail") and then painted him out of it.

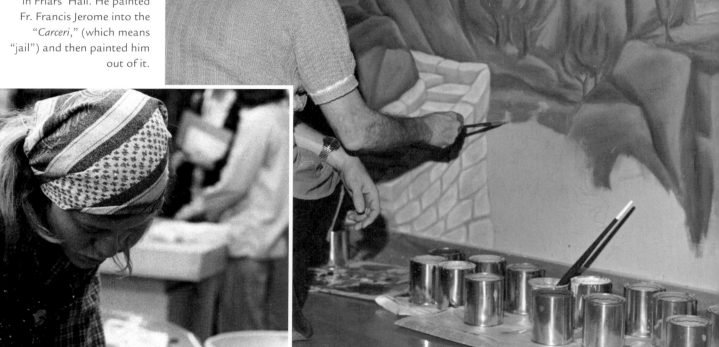

« In 1972, Fr. Tom Brown carved St. Joseph to match his carving of Mary.

Pottery has been a constant in the art program.

« In the early 1970s, painting murals on walls became popular. Students decorated all the stairway walls on the stairs near the president's office.

« Nancy Reagan was among many famous speakers who have appeared on campus over the years. This photo was taken in 1980.

« Senator Ted Kennedy spoke on campus during one of his campaigns.

» U.S. Representative Dick Durbin and Fr. Jim Toal listen to Senator Paul Simon campaign for the U.S. Senate in 1980.

« The QC Biology
Department did research
on the river both in summer
and in winter.

» Biology students
do field work at
Burton Creek in
October 1978.

« Fr. John Ostdiek and others in the biology program carried out government-sponsored research on the Mississippi River using this boat.

Dr. John Natalini taught biology from 1972 to 2006 and was responsible for helping numerous graduates get into medical school. Here he spends time with students in the "Cellar."

« Biology professor Dr. Al Pogge collects sap from a cottonwood tree in the river valley in 1976.

» Another legendary QC music professor was Charles ("Charlie") Winking. Here he directs the Presidential Concert in October 1978.

« The boar's head was the centerpiece of a madrigal dinner. Wassail had to also be part of the menu.

Dr. Louis ("Louie") Margaglione has taught music at QU since 1967.

Hugh Soebbing led QC jazz groups, such as this 1961 dance band, from his wheelchair. When he was not leading a group, he was usually monitoring the audio recording of the performance. The school constructed a homemade elevator in Solano Hall for his use.

» These two cooks at the Lind Street (Willer) Valentine bake sale in 1980 show Brenda Goeckner and Mary (Salrin) Betts at the stove.

Fr. Tom Brown taught class for years in his sport jacket and turtleneck shirt.

« Dr. David Costigan was hired in 1957 to coach baseball, and asked to teach history on the side. He taught from then until 2007. Late in his career, he received his doctorate from Illinois State University with an award-winning dissertation on Quincy's experience of the Civil War.

Fr. Owen Blum taught history from the 1940s until the 1980s. Fr. Francis Jerome calls him one of the "Four Horsemen" who shaped the College's development in the years after World War II. He was an internationally recognized authority on St. Peter Damian and edited many of his works for publication.

Centennial accommodations in the 1960s were not as colorful as today.

» The bell, dedicated in 1974 by Fr. Titus Ludes, honors an alumnus named Bill Scholten, who went on to graduate from West Point and was killed in a flying accident.

This 1980s view shows Penny Lane and Willer before Lind Street was closed.

» Fr. Tom Brown designed the kiosk when Penny Lane was extended to the south in 1983.

Another 1989 shot, perhaps of orientation, showing the solar screen on Friars' Hall in the background. The screen was removed in 2003 because of its deteriorating tiles.

A musical group entertains students on the A-field in the spring of 1989.

Fr. Tom Brown's sculpture, "Windows to the Future," was dedicated shortly before his death in 1994.

Sr. Ann Redig, O.S.F. served as campus minister from 1989 to 1996. Sharon Barnett has worked in graphic production for the University since shortly after her graduation from QC.

Dr. George Schneider was QC's resident ornithologist.

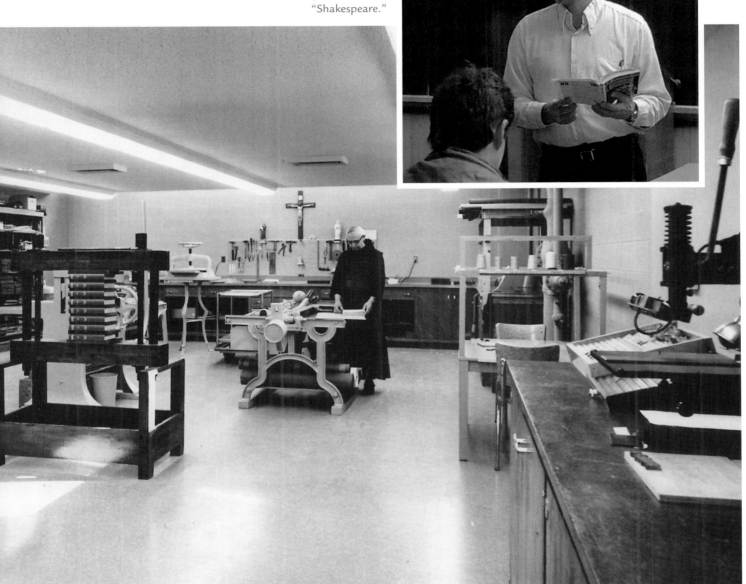

Dr. Joseph ("Joe") Messina taught English and served the College in many other capacities from 1975 until his retirement in 2008. The word "Math" behind him is not appropriate for his course matter—the sign should read "Shakespeare."

Br. Raymond Pohlmeyer was one of a series of friars who staffed a bookbindery in the basement of Brenner Library, using mostly nineteenth-century equipment. His work reduced the time needed for binding, making periodical issues more consistently available.

Today's Hawks' Hangout started as a student cafeteria,
became the College bookstore, and was finally
transformed into its present shape as an eating place.
This is what it looked like in its bookstore incarnation.

These 1989 *Falcon* readers must be either staff members from the paper or subjects of a *Falcon* article.

WWQC studio equipment in the early days was partially donated by local industries.

« Until the North Campus soccer field was created in the 1970s, QC varsity soccer was played on the baseball half of QU Stadium. Jack MacKenzie thinks this shot was taken during a 1973 NAIA playoff game against Wisconsin-Green Bay. Quincy won that game 1-0.

The centerpiece of the University mall was a fountain until the mechanics of it became unworkable.

The actor John Mahoney receives an honorary degree from Fr. Jim Toal.

Bill Dietrich was the University lawyer for many years. On the side, he taught the French horn, and practiced for hours in Solano.

Br. Clete Van Ackeren
honors his nephew's
graduation.

Return to Franciscan Roots
1997 to the Present

FR. JAMES TOAL IS NOT REMEMBERED FOR SUCH "SOFT" INITIATIVES as emphasizing the spiritual heritage of the school. Nevertheless, he ordered replicas of the San Damiano crucifix placed in each classroom, along with a description of the history and significance of the crucifix. Fr. James also gave Francis Hall its name; until his time, the building had been known simply as the administration building, or the "Ad Building." It was his successor, Fr. Eugene Kole, who arrived on campus with a reputation for "vision" and who placed the school's Franciscan tradition front and center.

THE CONVENTUALS

Over the centuries, since the time of Francis of Assisi (who died in 1226 C.E.), the Franciscan Order experienced as many reforms, secessions, and conflict as Protestantism, except that these conflicts took place within the fold of Roman Catholicism. Many of the conflicts revolved around the issue of poverty—do the friars live the lifestyle of Francis as "the poorest of the poor"? The tension goes back to the earliest years of the Order. Its earliest expression involved a movement that came to be called the "Spirituals." These men, who numbered among their group some of Francis's closest friends, preferred to live in very small communities, and came to draw inspiration from a Cistercian friar who lived a hundred years earlier, Joachim of Fiore.

Joachim saw the history of God's dealings with humanity as divided into three phases: the age of the Father (the Old Testament), the age of the Son (Christianity beginning with Jesus Christ), and the age of the Holy Spirit, which would begin shortly and would be announced by the coming of a new prophet. The Spirituals saw Francis as that new prophet. He was the one who was beginning the new age of the Spirit. Among the adherents of the Spiritualist movement was the Franciscan philosopher William of Ockham (of "Ockham's Razor" fame).

The Spirituals had the good fortune of having control of the public relations aspect of the Franciscan movement, especially through a series of stories that came to be called the "Little Flowers of St. Francis" (the *Fioretti*). These stories, which still shape popular images of the ideal Franciscan, fed later reforms down through the centuries.

Meanwhile, an alternate version of Franciscanism, which came to be called "Conventual," was taking over the majority of the men in the movement. The word "Conventual" refers to "convents," which meant larger houses (as opposed to the small houses of the Spirituals). St. Bonaventure was a leader of this movement, becoming general minister of the Order, rewriting the history of Francis's life (and ordering all earlier histories destroyed—an order which was fortunately disobeyed), and playing an important role in the life of the larger Church after he was made a cardinal.

By the late 1300s, the Conventuals themselves were giving birth to another reform movement from within, which came to be called "the Observance." The new movement peacefully reformed the Order from within, so that by the year 1500, the "Observants" had become the majority and the "Conventuals" a minority group within the Order.

Various other reforms sprang up over the years. In 1517, a movement that came to be called the "Capuchin" movement began. St. Peter of Alcantara (the spiritual director of Teresa of Avila) founded a rigorous movement called the Alcantarines. A group that came to be called the

« The lower grades at the All Students Mass sat on the gym floor.

An "All Students Mass," attended by children from all nearby Catholic grade and high schools and presided over by the Bishop of Springfield, has become an annual celebration.

"Recollects" became important in the history of Franciscans in the United States. Louis Hennepin, the discoverer of the Falls of St. Anthony in Minneapolis/St. Paul, was a Recollect, as were the friars who began Sacred Heart Province and Quincy College.

Finally, in 1897, Pope Leo XIII decided that the fragmentation had become dysfunctional, and he collapsed all the movements back into three groups: the Observants (the largest group—with the initials "O.F.M."), the Conventuals (O.F.M. Conv.), and the Capuchins (O.F.M. Cap.).

FR. EUGENE KOLE, O.F.M., CONV.

In 1987, the College Board had approved a rule change allowing a member of any of the main branches of the Order to be president of the College. Fr. Eugene Kole, who began his presidency of Quincy University in 1997, was a Conventual friar, the first friar not to be a member of the Observant branch. He had been praised as visionary, and he saw his role as one who could sketch out future directions for the University. Prior to accepting the presidency, Fr. Kole served as dean of graduate and continuing education and dean of enrollment management at Chestnut Hill College in Philadelphia, Pennsylvania. His installation as president was celebrated with great solemnity.

Fr. Eugene brought to completion a long-planned renovation of the gymnasium. The old gym was upgraded and a new fitness center was built to the west side of the older building. The entrance area to the campus was completely reconfigured, with a plaza and its centerpiece bronze statue of St. Francis. Despite these rapid expansion efforts, his "visionary" initiatives never came to fruition, creating feelings of disillusionment among the faculty and staff.

Within a few years, the University was floundering. The crisis came to a head with the 2001 visit of an accreditation team from the Higher Learning Commission (HLC) of the North Central Association. It refused to grant unconditional accreditation and required a follow-up "focus visit" of an HLC team in just three years, to focus on two areas: governance and assessment.

After concerns about the inconsistencies in his academic credentials grew, Fr. Kole resigned as president in October 2002 and was replaced by a Sacred Heart Province friar, Fr. Mario DiCicco, who accepted the post of interim president, which he held until June 2003.

FR. MARIO DICICCO

Fr. Mario was an energetic and gregarious man with two doctorates. He had taught English at the College in the early 1970s. He arrived on campus in January 2003 and immediately won praise for his opening the president's house to families of students who needed lodging when a student family member was hospitalized. He sponsored events with free food, declaring that he would pay for it out of his salary.

Serious work began in the task of responding to the HLC criticisms and demands for change. The eventual result was the formation of a permanent assessment committee, and the creation of the position of assessment research officer. A four-person faculty committee accepted responsibility for restructuring the governance of the University, and did impressive work in developing a new model of governance.

This 2005 photo shows the new Health and Fitness Center from Oak Street.

The 2001 fitness center construction included a complete redesign of the west end of the mall, featuring this bronze statue of St. Francis.

Four outstanding QU personalities were honored at the 2008 Commencement. Left to right, wearing caps: Dr. David Costigan, Charlene Peter, Jack MacKenzie, and John Ortwerth. Fr. Ken Capalbo, Board chair, and Dr. David Schachtsiek, interim president, pose with them.

Fr. Mario's role was envisioned as temporary, and the search for a permanent replacement began with the naming of a search committee and the hiring of a search firm. The Board of Trustees had loosened the requirements for the presidency of the school to include members of any Franciscan group, male or female. The opening to female candidates expanded the pool of potential applicants. There are at this writing at least nineteen Franciscan colleges and universities in the United States, only four of which are controlled by the Friars Minor, and most of which are owned by women religious.

Sister Margaret Feldner, O.S.F., a member of a group of Franciscan sisters based in Dubuque, Iowa, was selected to be the new president of the University. At the time, she was in charge of academics at Clarke College in Dubuque, an institution with an impressive standing in the *U.S. News and World Report* ranking.

SR. MARGARET FELDNER

Hopes were once again high as Sister Margaret assumed her position. Her official inauguration was more low-key than that of Fr. Kole, and featured an African American choir, reflecting her background as a member of an order that had worked with Franciscans of the Province at the African American Corpus Christi parish on Chicago's South Side.

Sr. Margaret continued to exemplify her idea of a Franciscan administrator. She picked up trash on her walks through the campus, visited student residences, and made attempts to improve the physical condition of those buildings. She attended athletic events faithfully. She hosted a tea for women students in her home, with the goal of connecting those students with influential women in the Quincy community.

Sr. Margaret made more explicit the goal of operationalizing the Catholic and Franciscan mission of the University. She exemplified in her own life the simplicity, concern for the environment, and solidarity with the poor that she saw as central Franciscan values. Perhaps the greatest tribute to her success is the way in which those who assumed control of QU after her departure, led by David Schachtsiek, based their actions on the desire to live out that mission.

The school had hired an admissions director who gave promise of turning around a perennial university problem, poor retention of entering freshmen. Unfortunately, the fall of 2005 and 2006 saw substantial drops in freshman enrollment. Sr. Margaret, by Christmas of 2006, was relieved of her duties and replaced by interim president Dr. David Schachtsiek.

The Franciscan Province of the Sacred Heart stood by the University throughout this period, investing considerable resources into its continuance, especially by building the new Holy Cross friary next to the campus on Twentieth Street, and by loaning the University substantial sums of money.

DR. DAVID SCHACHTSIEK

David Schachtsiek was a 1970 graduate of Quincy College. He had spent his career in several administrative positions in the Illinois correctional system, at St. John's Hospital in Springfield, and at Lincoln Land Community College in Springfield. He was hired to direct the adult education program, The Accelerated University (TAU) program.

Dr. Schachtsiek came to Quincy with the hope of combining service to his alma mater with an intellectually stimulating retirement. The retirement aspect did not last long. By 2003, he was vice president for academic affairs, and when Sr. Margaret departed, he assumed responsibility for the school as interim president.

The first thing Dr. Schachtsiek and his colleagues did was to hire a professional firm

« Sr. Margaret takes part in a celebration of a second Chicago-to-Quincy daily train schedule. Amtrack service to Quincy has been an important service to the University over the years.

to coach the admissions staff, with the goal of improving enrollment. Their efforts were successful, as Quincy achieved a 26-percent increase in new student enrollment in the fall of 2007, a 10-percent increase in the fall of 2008, and another 11-percent increase in the fall of 2009, including the largest incoming class in twelve years.

Syndi Peck, originally hired to teach TAU Human Services courses, had been promoted to director of the entire program of TAU. She stepped in to help in the recruiting effort, and was so successful that she was offered and accepted the job of full-time director of admissions.

The consultant offered many useful suggestions that contributed to the University's success. One was to strategically utilize the director of computing, David Moore. Among other contributions, Moore was able to allow the school to replace an expensive course management software system with his own construction, which was both financially beneficial and user-friendly.

The Board of Trustees hired a professional search firm to look for a new president. During Sr. Margaret's tenure, the Board had removed the "Franciscan only" restriction from the bylaws criteria for president, which provided a much larger pool of applicants with competitive credentials.

The search process went forward, with a goal of having a new president on board by the summer of 2008. Four candidates were selected for interview. All four were extensively interviewed. The final choice was Dr. Robert Gervasi.

DR. ROBERT GERVASI

Dr. Gervasi joined Quincy University in June of 2008 as the University's twenty-second president and first lay president. He was selected by the Board because of his combined experience and leadership of over thirty years in higher education, business, and Franciscan life. Most recently he had been president of the Institute for Study Abroad, an educational organization that prepares and places American students for study in universities internationally.

He spent his first summer living with the friars in the friary to get a good feel for the Franciscan spirit of Quincy University. Shortly after his arrival, Quincy University's Franciscan caring spirit became evident during the Mississippi River flood. During the crisis, Dr. Gervasi opened the campus to Illinois National Guard members, who utilized the Health and Fitness Center as housing, and the American Red Cross, who utilized the first floor of Friars' Hall as its base and Centennial Hall as temporary housing for victims.

During the next year, Dr. Gervasi upheld the promise of a bright future for Quincy University. With the start of the 2009 school year, the University

Dr. Robert Gervasi was inaugurated as Quincy University's twenty-second president and first lay president. The theme of his inaugural address was "Higher Learning, Franciscan Living."

David Schachtsiek, Greg Warren, Diane Frese, and Crystal Sutter share lunch at Frank 'n Clare's.

found itself marking its 150th year with an 11-percent enrollment increase in the fall semester. The University community also prepared for a comprehensive review for accreditation by the Higher Learning Committee (HLC) of the North Central Association of Colleges and Schools to ensure that the University was effectively fulfilling its educational mission. The visit proved to be a notable success, resulting in the recommendation that Quincy University be reaccredited for ten years—the maximum period allowed.

Dr. Gervasi continued to further guide the University to success in 2009, when the Board of Trustees approved the construction of a new student residence hall that would be the first on the campus in thirty-five years. Plans for the residence hall include the accommodation of ninety-two students after its completion with the expected groundbreaking to take place in the spring of 2010, with completion and occupancy planned for the fall of 2011.

Perhaps one of the more significant outcomes of Dr. Gervasi's continued implementation of the Franciscan spirit in higher learning came in the form of the 50 State Service Project, a mission spearheaded by two Campus Ministry graduate assistants under the direction of Fr. John Doctor and Br. Ed Arambasich in celebration of the University's 150th anniversary. The project operates under the plan to send small groups of students, faculty, staff, and alumni to work in each of the fifty states by the end of the academic year, focusing on the ministry of presence. Those involved will engage in extensive networking across the country, thereby laying the groundwork for an ongoing expansion of Quincy University's service initiatives.

The articulation of realistic and forward-looking goals, within the Franciscan spirit, is a central theme of this book. Our future is in good hands.

Sandbagging in a flood emergency brings many people together in a shared enterprise.

The Mississippi River flooded seriously in 2008, causing an emergency sandbagging operation to be mounted at the Quincy Civic and Convention Center. QU students joined in the effort.

« Mass for alumni gatherings has always been a regular feature of the events.

⌄ Fr. Ralph Parthie preaches at a recent mass for alumni.

Sr. Margaret and two students get Francis suited up for a March 2005 event celebrating QU's basketball successes.

Basketball coach Marty Bell watches the action with his players in a recent game.

Dr. Bob Gervasi and his wife Jen took part in a fall 2008 event.

Each fall, athletes from all QU sports meet in the chapel for a "Blessing of the Athletes."

Catching the bus to or from class at North Campus can play havoc with arriving to class in time. The class schedule had to be changed to allow fifteen minutes between classes. Even that was not always enough time to get from one campus to the other.

⌃ Fr. Carlos Ruiz
and Syndi Peck
discuss HLC
matters.

« Students talk
with Fr. Carlos
Ruiz on the mall
during the fall
of 2008.

In the summer of 2007, Brenner
Library received a new coat
of paint designed to make
the building blend with its
neighbors, especially the Health
and Fitness Center.

A student volunteer displays a saying attributed to St. Francis: "Preach the Gospel at all times; when necessary, use words."

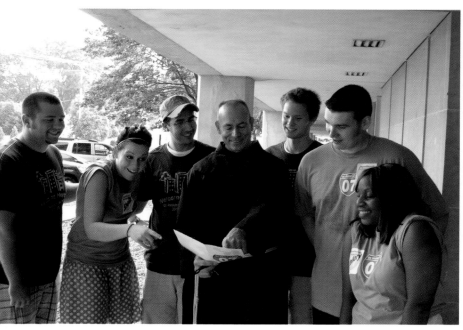

Br. Ed Arambasich shows an important document to several students at the Padua entrance in this 2007 picture.

Br. Ed leads students from St. Francis School on a tour through Francis Hall at Halloween. The objective, of course, is to harvest candy from FRH offices.

As chaplain to the Quincy Fire Department, Br. Ed sponsors a blessing of firefighters and their equipment each year.

« Football games can draw big crowds, especially at Homecoming time.

The game begins.

Volleyball is a more athletic sport than this author remembers.

Dr. David Robinson has taught computer science since 1994.

Dr. Ekemezie ("Joe") Emeka has taught mathematics at QU since 1990.

« Fr. Philibert Hoebing has the distinction of having served at Quincy College longer than any other Franciscan. He joined the faculty in 1953 and still lives in Holy Cross Friary.

⟝ Bob Mejer poses with some of his art students.

Dr. Cynthia Haliemun teaches economics in the School of Business. She joined the QU staff in 1999.

» Paul Meyer and Pat Laytham converse at a 2005 gathering.

Sr. Margaret shares a laugh with Jack MacKenzie and Pat Atwell during her fiftieth jubilee celebration as a Franciscan sister.

Fr. Phil's fiftieth priestly anniversary was celebrated by his receiving a plaza brick. Left to right: Fr. Irenaeus Kimminau, Joe Winkelmann, Br. Joe Manning, Dr. John Schleppenbach, Fr. Phil, Fr. Joe Zimmerman, Judy Winkelmann, Rev. Paul Schwartzkopf, Alex the friary mascot, Fr. Ralph Parthie, and Br. Ed Arambasich.

« Nick Ruhs and Bridget Quinlivan share conversation with Dr. Mary Ann Klein at a 2008 honors dinner. Over the years, Mary Ann and her husband Dr. Joe Messina have used their home to host innumerable celebrations for students, honoring their achievements.

≫ Not all games
are won.

» A November club expo is designed to make students aware of campus activity groups.

⌄ Quincy Catholic Charities, whose present director is a QU alumnus, sponsors a fundraiser each spring featuring a walk/run across the two Mississippi River bridges at Quincy. Dr. Gervasi took part in the spring 2008 run.

« Students volunteer at a Habitat for Humanity site.

≫ Students do service work in St. Louis under the direction of Franciscan Connection, an agency which provides in-kind help to an inner-city neighborhood.

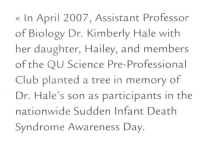

« In April 2007, Assistant Professor of Biology Dr. Kimberly Hale with her daughter, Hailey, and members of the QU Science Pre-Professional Club planted a tree in memory of Dr. Hale's son as participants in the nationwide Sudden Infant Death Syndrome Awareness Day.

Ken Medo, Yazmin Pulido, Katrina Schroeder, and T. J. Standberry showcase Francis Hall in this 2008 photo.

An August 2008 group of students are enjoying something.

Tailgating is a tradition that QU alums continue.

Athletics continue to provide meaningful experiences for students.

The women's 2007 softball team.

Pulitzer Prize-winning author James B. Stewart, a native of Quincy, is a frequent visitor to the University.

Judy Winkelmann, who recently finished her degree at QU and now manages the Quincy Historical Society, is shown with Ben Bumbry, now an alderman on the Quincy City Council. Mr. Bumbry was one of the 1950s players coached by Harry Forrester.

Pat Atwell, former baseball coach and QU athletic director, shakes hands with Josh Kinney, a QU graduate who went on to pitch for the St. Louis Cardinals in the World Series.

Dr. Bill Postiglione points out things to Julie Bell at the HLC Conference.

Solano was demolished in the summer of 2008.

Janet Peters takes part in campus clean-up day activities.

« A room in Garner is somewhat more colorful than its counterpart in Padua.

⌄ This room in Padua, like its counterpart in Garner, was probably cleaned up for public display.

Women's soccer continues to excel as an athletic program today.

The 2006 club fair featured a display for the Phi Sigma Sigma sorority.

Music continues at QU, as in this 2007 performance in the chapel.

QU's SIFE Club (Students in Free Enterprise) has consistently ranked well in competition around the state and country. In this 2004 picture, students are flanked by Dr. Mitch Ellison on the left and Dr. Cynthia Haliemun on the right.

A "right to life" display is part of a club fair, an opportunity for student groups to present their case to the public.

« Former women's basketball coach Larry Just passed on a tradition of coaching excellence to his successor, J. D. Gravina.

» Jack MacKenzie watches the action at a 1998 game. This scene has been repeated since the 1960s, when he took control of QC's soccer program. Over the years, he has coached his players to academic, athletic, and spiritual excellence.

Freshmen students spell out their new school's initials during orientation.

Jerry Peters and Dave Schullian retired from the QU Maintenance Department in 2005.

QU students work with children at St. Francis grade school.

Sue (Rummenie) Winking does kitchen work for the semi-annual "late night breakfast," during which faculty and staff serve breakfast to students at 11 p.m. on the night before final exams begin.

Buildings and Grounds

THE NEW AMERICAN BIBLE TRANSLATION OF VERSES 15-16 OF PSALM 103 says: "Our days are like the grass... we are gone; [and] our place knows us no more." Buildings outlast the men and women who inhabit them. They serve as anchors of history and memory. The buildings of Quincy College can stir reminiscences and reflection on the experiences of all those who have lived and worked here before us.

FIRST BUILDINGS: 1860 TO 1871

As was noted in the first chapter, Quincy College began in a storefront at Eighth and Maine streets. The bottom floor was a classroom, the second floor was living quarters for the friars, and the third floor was a chapel. (Since there were no boarding students, presumably the friars were the only ones who would use the third floor.)

None of the buildings of 1860 are standing today. The first St. Francis Church was located on the site of the present chapel. The church, slightly shorter than the present college chapel, was architecturally deficient. The walls would not bear the weight of the roof, so iron rods and brick buttresses had to be added to save the building from collapse.

The new friary, east and a bit north of the church, was a two-story brick building with fourteen rooms. The western part of the first floor contained two classrooms, while the eastern half served as a temporary chapel until the church was completed.

By January 1861, the friars had moved to rooms in the newly constructed St. Aloysius Orphanage at Twentieth and College (then called Vine Street), where they taught until February 1865, when the Orphanage Society reclaimed the building. By that time, the parish had built a parochial school on the corner of Eighteenth and Vine, and the College operated from rooms in that building until 1871, when the present east wing of Francis Hall was built.

The present east wing features many chimneys, no doubt because there was no central heating when it was built, and each room needed its own stove. It is interesting that one chimney is missing on the west half of the north side of that wing. This was because the northwest area of the first floor was a dining hall, and the same area of the second floor was a study hall—both larger spaces which presumably did not need as many heating stoves. Meals for the friars and boarders were cooked in the friary building next door.

The top floor of the east wing was used as a dormitory for boarding students. Before its renovation, home-built "lockers" could be seen in the wainscoting of the walls of the fourth floor in that wing.

One peculiar fact is that an architectural drawing of Francis Hall, framed in the corridor outside the president's office and used in the college catalogs for several years beginning in 1894–1895, shows the east wing with four complete stories above the basement level. That wing actually has only three stories above the basement level. The same drawing shows the tower with clocks; Fr. Francis Jerome says that clocks were never installed, but the openings were filled by stained glass windows until those windows deteriorated and had to be removed in the 1930s. New glass windows were installed and dedicated in August 2009 in preparation for the 150-year anniversary in 2010. The glass windows are brightly lit during the evening.

PLUMBING

Not only was central heating non-existent in 1871, but central plumbing was also not well developed. The roof of many buildings of that period, including the east wing of the College, contained a water tank, designed to be pumped full and used for continuous water flow in the rooms below. (The tank on the east wing was disguised to look like a steeple.) A separate building, nicknamed the "Dunnigan," was

« This part of the east wing is now occupied by classrooms FRH 403 and the faculty lounge.

Below: This picture was taken around 1912 in front of the "Dunnigan" (toilet building), about where the entrance to Friars' Hall is now located. The building in the background is the now-demolished study hall/ auditorium.

constructed just north of Francis Hall, about where the walkway now connects Francis Hall with Friars' Hall, to serve as a restroom for larger numbers of men.

THE WALL

At first the College operated on the square block between College, Elm, Eighteenth Street, and the nonexistent Nineteenth Street. When Fr. Nicholas Leonard added the study hall/auditorium to the east wing in 1895, the College bought some land from the Orphanage Society, and eventually bought the rest of the space between the college building and Twentieth Street. When the Orphanage Society built a new building (Solano Hall) across College Avenue in 1918, the old orphanage building was demolished and the present athletic field came into existence.

In 1919-1920, Fr. Gabriel Lucan built a stone wall around the entire two square blocks of the then-existing campus. The College Avenue portion of the wall was removed when the street was closed by Fr. Gabriel Brinkman in 1966. When Fr. James Toal closed Elm Street in 1984, most of the wall along Elm Street was removed and pieces of it were used to reconstruct the wall to close off both Elm and College on the east side of the building.

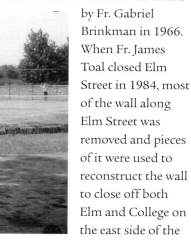

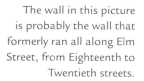
The wall in this picture is probably the wall that formerly ran all along Elm Street, from Eighteenth to Twentieth streets.

When this writer climbed to the top of the tower of Francis Hall some years ago, he was surprised to see students' names carved into the stones capping the walls there. How could students have been able to spend enough time on the tower to carve their names? Then the answer came: those stones must have been part of a wall along the street. At some point their portion of the wall was removed, and the stones were used to cap the tower brickwork when modifications were made to the tower!

THE TOWER

The original central section of Francis Hall was capped by a short steeple on the present tower. The steeple was removed shortly after the chapel was completed in 1912. Fr. Francis Jerome says the architect overshot his abilities when designing it. While the steeple of St. Francis Church, built in 1884, is still standing, several other churches built by Br. Adrian Wewer featured steeples that had to be removed, including Blessed Sacrament Church in Quincy and St. Joseph Church in Palmyra, Missouri. When work was being done in the tower area during the 1960s or 1970s, steel reinforcements had to be built into the structure, because parts of the brickwork were resting on wooden support beams.

THE ROOT CELLAR

In 1919, Fr. Gabriel Lucan constructed a root cellar, built into the wall along Eighteenth Street. The cellar became a garage when the friars got their first automobiles, "war surplus" cars, in 1947. For a brief period, the building became a kiln for firing ceramics for the Art Department. For many years, the friar cooks served meals for transients in this building; a similar structure built into the wall of the parish across Eighteenth Street served the same purpose.

QU-STADIUM

The story of QU-Stadium began in 1923, when the Quincy Aerie of Eagles bought the land and used it for a baseball field. The Quincy Public Schools bought the property in 1937, and in 1938, a grant from the WPA (Works Progress Administration—a New Deal anti-Depression project) allowed the present stadium to be built, using stone from the local river bottoms. The structure got the nickname "The Rock Pile," a prison allusion not helped by barbed wire security strands that topped its walls.

Over the years, the stadium was home to several minor league baseball teams. Some famous names in baseball played here are: Hank Bauer, Lew Burdette, Whitey Herzog, and Tony Kubek. From 1946 to 1954, the New York Yankees farm team played here, the San Francisco Giants from 1960 to 1961, the New York Mets in 1961–1962, and the Chicago Cubs from 1963 to 1973. During most of these years, the Quincy team was known as the Gems.

From 1974 to 1987, the field was used by the Central Illinois Collegiate League (CICL), with a team named the Rivermen.

In 1980, the Quincy Public Schools sold the field to the city of Quincy, which in turn sold it to Quincy College for one dollar in 1984.

Since 1996, the field has been the home to a CICL (now Prospect League) team named the Gems, under the auspices of the Oakley-Lindsay Civic Center Authority. That organization invested considerable resources in developing the baseball half of the field into a much more attractive place, and Quincy University has benefited from these improvements as our own baseball team continues to use the field. The football half of the area, the home of the Hawks since the College resumed football in the mid-1980s, has seen less renovation, and is still in need of serious repairs.

THE BROWER ENGINEERING BUILDING

Fr. Erhard Kuester almost single-handedly created an engineering program on campus in the early 1940s, and the Brower family contributed money to construct a two-story building on the present site of Friars' Hall in which the program operated. Fr. Erhard had tried to build a full four-year major program in engineering, but accrediting agencies required that its offerings be limited to a two-year pre-engineering curriculum. The program survived Fr. Erhard's death in 1967, and

was briefly resurrected as a four-year degree under the sponsorship of Fr. Eugene Kole, but was again cut back to the two-year version soon after his departure, when funding for a full program failed to materialize. The Brower building itself was demolished in 1963 to make room for Friars' Hall.

THE "CAMP ON THE BAY"

Some time in the 1960s, the College acquired a camp built on Quincy Bay, on property formerly owned by an ice company. (Cutting ice from the Bay during winter was an important business in the days before refrigeration became common.) Shortly after the College acquired the camp, it burned. Br. Richard Hoffman, director of the Maintenance Department, was able to build a newer building of brick and steel, raised high enough to be safe from flooding (until the flood of 1993, which reached three or four feet into the upper floor of the structure).

Over several years, Fr. Tom Brown and others renovated the upstairs of the camp, decorating the stairway with carved railings and the fireplace with a mantel and supports carved from great logs. The building was used by College personnel for picnics and other celebrations—"whole hog dinners" for the entire faculty and "wild game dinners" sponsored especially by Fr. Phil Hoebing and Br. Clete Van Ackeren.

Br. Clete had been given a pontoon boat by a relative, and he used the boat for outings for friars, faculty, and friends who wanted boat rides on the Mississippi. As Quincy Bay gradually silted in, it became more difficult to launch the boat from the camp, and after Br. Clete's death in 1991 the boat was sold.

In the 1970s, the camp was sold by the College to the friars, and in 1994, the University bought it back, intending to use it as a "Life Science Field Station and Conference Center." Periodic flooding has always made the use of the camp an "iffy" proposition. A few years ago the University again sold it.

another was for a time the home of Dr. David and Mary Costigan and their family.

THE COLLEGE SWITCHBOARD, MAIL ROOM, AND FACULTY LOUNGE

For years, the College switchboard and mail room were located in the space just to the right as you enter Francis Hall via the main entrance.

Br. Clete and a series of laywomen staffed the switchboard. Br. Clete acted as College contact during the night hours. The College phone system was set up to ring in Br. Clete's room on the seventh floor of Friars' Hall whenever a call came in for anyone in the friary or College, and for years he carried this responsibility without complaint.

The switchboard area was divided by a windowed partition from the mail room, where plywood boxes allowed anyone to place mail into a faculty member's box and to take mail from it. Across the hallway, on the left side of the main entrance, was a faculty lounge, where faculty could share coffee and conversation. Fr. James Toal moved the mailroom to the basement location where locked boxes now make faculty mail more secure, and moved the faculty lounge to the east end of the fourth floor, an attractive space, but one whose location is not conducive to casual gathering. He converted the switchboard/mail room to a sitting room for the Admissions Department, and the lounge area into an administrative office.

Student houses survive near the west end of Lind Street.

ON-CAMPUS HOUSES

The construction of the residence halls has been described in other places in this book. Many students have fond memories of living in what had been private homes, purchased by the University over the years, and often demolished to make room for other uses. There were rows of houses along Oak Street west of the gymnasium, and on Eighteenth Street north of Oak, in which students lived. There had been houses along Elm Street before it was closed, and along the south side of Lind Street. The north side of Lind Street still preserves some of these houses, as does the east side of Eighteenth Street north of Lind. Houses on the site of Holy Cross Friary and the tennis courts on Twentieth Street were homes to students for many years. Many of these houses can be seen in aerial photos of the College taken at various times.

Many years ago, before this writer's arrival in Quincy, there were houses along College Avenue across the street from Francis Hall. One of those houses served as the College bookstore, and

FRIARS' HALL AND HOLY CROSS FRIARY

Ever since the first buildings of the College were built, the friars lived in the College building. Up until the 1950s, when over thirty friars were stationed here, the western part of Francis Hall was the friars' living quarters. Most friars had private rooms on the second and third floors. A recreation room on the third floor, in the large space above what is now the FRH 240 computer lab, a space formerly used by the Reading Center, was complemented by a dumb waiter used to bring drinks (beer) up from the basement on *Spielabend* nights. (The German term means "play evening.") The friars' dining room was on the north end of the first floor of the west wing. The student dining room took up the entire west side of that floor, except for the kitchen, which was between the student and the friar dining rooms.

As the number of friars in the Province grew, it became clear that the College would need more space to house friar faculty. Friars' Hall was built and financed from government loans. It was designed to house sixty men, twelve on a floor, with a dining room and recreation room on the second floor, a tailor shop, guest rooms, and parlors on the first floor, and utility rooms in the basement.

Early in 1979, the south third of the roof over the walkway connecting Friars' Hall with Francis Hall collapsed. The roof had been attached to the wall of the garage with bolts, and the bolts rusted through.

Friars' Hall, which for most of its history was known simply as "the Friary," or by some as "the friar Hilton," featured a solar screen made of tile covering the entire building. By 2003, the tiles had

begun to crack and were removed lest they become a hazard to passersby on the ground below.

Over the years, the number of friars dropped below twenty, and the Province, after study, concluded that the building was too large for our needs and that the friars should look for other accommodations. After discussing the possibility of buying buildings somewhere else in the city, the friars decided that it was important to remain near the campus, and the Province agreed to build a new friary on land purchased from the University for one dollar. Province administrators

Friars' Hall looks more open, now that the solar screen has been removed.

in St. Louis made all the important decisions, hiring the Quincy architectural firm of Architechnics, Inc. to design the facility, and making the decision to install geothermal heating, reflecting an increasing Franciscan emphasis on environmental conservation. The new set of two buildings was complete by the summer of 2002, and the friars moved that summer. Friars' Hall became a student residence, with administrative offices on the first floor.

The new friary has been seen by almost all observers as a beautiful and practical substitute for what had become a much too institutional setting for friar life. An unexpected benefit was

Holy Cross Friary was completed in 2002 and can accommodate fourteen friars.

the construction of a covered patio between the two buildings, which has become a delightful space to be used all through the warmer months of the year.

THE NORTH CAMPUS

By the early 1960s, the Franciscan Province "minor seminary," a six-year program encompassing four years of high school and two years of college, was outgrowing its 1927 building in Oak Brook, Illinois. The Province mounted a capital campaign and built a new facility, Our

Lady of Angels Seminary, at Eighteenth Street and Seminary Road. The two years of college were moved here from Oak Brook, and a three-year program in philosophy was moved from Cleveland. Tradition in the Province had been that after the two years of college at Oak Brook, the candidate for the Order would move to Teutopolis, Illinois, where he would receive the Franciscan habit and spend a year as a novice. After that year, he would go to Cleveland for three more years. At the end of the five years of college, he would receive a degree of Bachelor of Arts in Philosophy from Quincy College. Friars educated under this system, including this writer, never set foot in Quincy, but we are included in the alumni lists of Quincy College.

The new Quincy seminary was designed to preserve the social distance between pre-novitiate and post-novitiate students. The pre-novitiate students lived in the "B-wing" along Seminary Road, and had their own dining room. The post-novitiate students lived in the "D-wing," which also had its own dining room. The two groups shared a chapel which had sliding doors in the middle that could be opened or closed, depending on whether the groups were to be separate or combined for religious events. The D-wing students had air conditioning, reflecting the reality that they would stay in Quincy over the summer, while the pre-novitiate students would be off-campus and in their hometowns.

No sooner had the new building been completed and dedicated in 1964, than the bottom fell out of the seminary population all over the country. Soon the number of seminarians had declined so much that the Province decided to welcome seminarians studying for the diocesan priesthood in several dioceses: Springfield, Belleville, Joliet, Rockford, and Springfield/Cape Girardeau were some. This temporarily boosted enrollment, but by the mid-1970s, this system was beginning to break down, partly because bishops in those dioceses began to pull their candidates out of the Quincy facility, and partly because the Province wanted to gear its program specifically to Franciscan candidates rather than adapt to diocesan customs. In the meantime, the high school seminary, which had remained at Oak Brook, was suffering a similar decline in enrollment and was closed by the Province in 1977.

The seminary authorities made valiant efforts to use the building during the 1970s. At one point during the late 1970s, John Wood Community College was renting the "A-wing" for its administrative offices, Cheryl Loatsch was using a room on the west end of the D-wing as a dance studio, and the Quincy Public Schools were running an alternative school for troubled students in the basement of the B-wing.

By the mid-1980s, the Province had decided to phase out its Quincy program. It sold the facility to Quincy College for a nominal sum. The acquisition made it possible for Fr. James Toal to move the chemistry, biology, physics, and psychology programs to the seminary building, which he renamed the North Campus. This opened up the east end of the fourth floor of Francis Hall, where biology had been located, and allowed Fr. James to tear down the chemistry building between Friars' Hall and the Hawks' Hangout building. The physics program area, which had been located on the fourth floor in the tower section of Francis Hall, became meeting rooms for the Board of Trustees.

WHAT MIGHT HAVE BEEN

Fr. Loyola Knoblauch, this writer's theology teacher and later chaplain at the Illinois Veterans' Home, described an offer made to the Province by an unknown donor of a piece of property near Camp Point, Illinois, where the new seminary could have been built. Fr. Loyola lamented the decision to build in Quincy. In his view, the Province turned down an offer of a piece of property near a beautiful lake in favor of a piece of land "between a railroad, an asphalt plant, and a cemetery." He had a point. Not only was

the seminary boxed in by those less desirable neighbors, but it was built on what was said to be a landfill, which required the entire building to be supported by pilings under the building's footings. Of course, had the Province decided to build the seminary in Camp Point, it would have been impossible for the building to be of use to the College.

THE DIACONATE PROGRAM

Around 2002, the University completed an agreement with the Catholic Diocese of Springfield, Illinois, to educate candidates for the permanent diaconate. The diocese had never made provisions for such education, and had no deacons beyond those who had moved to the diocese from elsewhere; the newly appointed bishop, Bishop George Lucas, changed the policy. The program was designed to be completed over four years, and was housed at the North Campus. At the request of the diocese, the University developed a master's program in theology.

In 2007, the diocese announced that it had decided to contract with St. Meinrad Seminary in St. Meinrad, Indiana, to educate its deacon candidates.

Today's North Campus started out as Our Lady of Angels Seminary.

SOCCER AND SOFTBALL

The acquisition of North Campus had further benefits for the College. It allowed the College to construct a state-of-the-art soccer field, with lighting supplied in 1976 through the generosity of Bernie and Isabelle Willer. The Willers were longtime supporters of the College, whose generosity was recognized by the University's naming of the Lind Street Dorm as Willer Hall in 1993.

Some years later, in 2005, the College built its new softball stadium west of the soccer field, ending a long period during which women's softball had to be played at a facility on the far northwest edge of the city area. The new stadium was named the Mart Heinen Softball Complex in recognition of the financial support of the Mart Heinen Club.

WWQC AND WQUB

Radio began at Quincy College in the late 1940s, with a tiny transmitter designed to be received only on campus. During the 1970s, under the direction of Connie Joe Mason, the station was named WWQC, placed its antenna on the tower of Francis Hall, and broadcast with a power level of 10 watts, enabling it to be heard throughout the city of Quincy. Under the leadership of Fr. Harry Speckman, who forged ties with local firms such as Broadcast Electronics and Harris Corporation, both of which make broadcasting equipment and

have supported the station by generous donations of equipment and talent, the station increased its power and expanded its coverage. In 1988, Fr. Harry began an alliance with National Public Radio, or NPR, an alliance which reached full NPR partnership status in 1994.

In the early 1990s, the station was able to build the present 420-foot tower on the North Campus property, and increase its power to 100,000 watts, which gave the station impressive coverage to the west and south of Quincy. A ridge of land east of Quincy has prevented stations from further east, especially the University of Illinois at Springfield, which maintains a transmitter in Pike County, from broadcasting to the city of Quincy.

When the University changed its name from Quincy College in 1993, the station changed its call letters to WQUB. Since then it has continued to expand its office space on the second floor of Francis Hall. More recently it has begun to broadcast digitally, a capability which allows it

The year 2004 saw the creation of QU's own softball field, the Mart Heinen Softball Complex.

« Before the University changed its name in 1992, its radio station was called "WWQC."

to provide twenty-four-hour offerings in specific interest areas, such as jazz music and news.

The University has maintained consistent financial support of the station, support on the order of $100,000 per year, in order to keep the station on the air.

THE FRANCISCAN PRESS

The Franciscan Province had begun a magazine before 1920 called *The Franciscan Herald*, a magazine that had attained national circulation for a brief period. The national circulation declined and the journal was combined with a journal supporting the Franciscan "Third Order" (now renamed the "Secular Franciscan Order"— S.F.O.), and renamed the *Franciscan Herald and Forum*. Under the leadership of Fr. Mark Hegener, a leadership which amounted to a one-man show, the journal became a publishing house which published a series of somewhat idiosyncratic titles, the most notable of which was some of the early writing of the present Pope, Benedict XVI.

After Fr. Mark's death, Fr. Gabriel Brinkman took over as press manager, but after a few years he moved on, and the neighborhood where the Press offices were located in Chicago became blighted. The Province closed the parish church and school there and sold the property. Fr. James Toal acquired the Press and its stock of published

materials, thirteen semi-truck-loads of inventory, and had the operation moved to Quincy. He relocated the Press office in houses on campus, first in a house on what was formerly Lind Street, then in a house on the corner of Eighteenth and Lind, and finally in Friars' Hall in what had been the friars' tailor shop. Dr. Terrence Riddell had managed the Press on a part-time basis. Jaime Vidal was hired as a full-time manager, and held that post until Fr. Eugene Kole decided that the University could no longer afford to pay a full-time manager. After his departure, the Press functioned solely as a distributor of materials published in the past.

In 2006, the University made the decision to phase out the entire Press operation. Under the leadership of the Rev. Mr. Leo Bistak, who also managed the North Campus facility and directed the diaconate formation program there, the Press was dissolved and its inventory parceled out to other places. Some of the more scholarly publications were acquired by the Franciscan Institute at St. Bonaventure University in upstate New York, and the more popular ones by the St. Anthony Messenger Press in Cincinnati. A few were acquired by other presses under a "publish on demand" arrangement, whereby each copy is printed as demand requires, thus eliminating the need to maintain an inventory of unsold books.

In the summer of 2008, the garage space formerly used to store Press books was converted into shower and locker space for the football team, which had begun to practice on the athletic field. The new Mart Heinen Softball Complex at North Campus had eliminated the space the football team formerly used for practice.

A Timeline of Significant Events

February 1860 – Classes begin in building at Eighth and Maine

February 1861 – Classes taught in St. Aloysius Orphanage at Twentieth and Vine

Early 1860s – St. Francis Solanus parish school, church, and friary built on the corner of Eighteenth and Vine (renamed College Avenue in 1926); school is on corner, church on site of present College chapel, friary northeast of church

1865 – College classes taught in rooms in parish school

1871 – Classes begin in new building, now the easternmost wing of Francis Hall

1873 – College granted charter by the state of Illinois to grant degrees of Bachelor of Arts and Master of Arts

1878 – Augustus Tolton, who was to become the first publicly known black priest in the United States, enters the College as student

1886 – New St. Francis Church and Friary completed on west side of Eighteenth Street; old friary converted into chapel

1893 – Study hall/auditorium wing on east side of Francis Hall begun (demolished in 1983)

1894 – Western wing of Francis Hall begun

1898 – Middle section of Francis Hall, including tower, completed

1909 – Commercial department, resembling bank office, moves into southwest corner of Francis Hall (now WQUB offices)

1911 – Bowling alleys completed under study hall

1912 – Chapel dedicated

1917 – College name changed from St. Francis Solanus College to Quincy College and Seminary

1918 – New orphanage opened on south side of College Avenue; College purchases land of old orphanage and demolishes it to make athletic field

1918 – First evening classes

1919–1920 – Wall around campus built

1922 – Steam laundry (Cupertine Hall) built

1922 – University of Illinois accredits College as a junior college

1922 – First woman, a religious sister, admitted

1926 – City renames Vine Street as College Avenue

1929 – The *Falcon* begins publication

1930 – European six-year program replaced by four years of high school (called the "Academy" at the time) and two years of junior college

1932 – Women first admitted as full-time day students

1933 – College accredited by University of Illinois to offer two-year and four-year college degrees

1933–1939 – College survives Depression years by laying off all but two lay faculty, turning off heat in half of the radiators and in the chapel, and discontinuing all periodical subscriptions

1940 – High school program (the "Academy") dropped; high school boys in Quincy henceforth would be educated along with girls at Notre Dame Academy at Eighth and Broadway

1941 – College acquires Stillwell Hall (now the Quincy Museum) at Sixteenth and Maine as a donation

1941–1945 – World War II greatly reduces male College enrollment; College survives by training naval cadets and army reservists

1942 – College discontinues baseball and basketball

1946 – Revival of enrollment begins with return of veterans from World War II, funded by the G.I. Bill

1946 – College acquires St. Aloysius Orphanage (Solano Hall), and houses students in eight war surplus barracks on site of present Centennial Hall as well as in buildings off campus, including Stillwell and Bonfoey Halls

1946 – Mart Heinen, College athletic director, and three City of Quincy officials die of smoke inhalation during the Chicago LaSalle Hotel fire; Heinen and the officials were in Chicago to raise money

1946 – College announces its first expansion drive; eventually $225,000 is collected

1946 – Intercollegiate athletics resume

1946 – Two buildings from munitions factories in Illiopolis, Illinois, moved to campus; one, west of Friars' Hall, was used for the chemistry program; the second,

the building now known as the Hawks' Hangout, was originally a cafeteria

1946 – The St. Aloysius Orphan Society building purchased and renamed Solano Hall (demolished in 2008)

1947 – Fr. Erhard Kuester begins engineering program in Brower building

1947 – First annual "vocation institute" held under direction of Fr. Pacific Hug

1947 – Quarterback Club (now Mart Heinen Club) established

1948 – Quincy College Foundation created, the beginning of the College endowment

1948 – First attempt to get North Central Association accreditation fails

1948 – Drive for a new gymnasium begins: over $300,000 collected

1950 – Gymnasium dedicated

1953 – Major fire on fourth floor of Francis Hall nearly burns down the building

1954 – Varsity football discontinued

1954 – College achieves first accreditation by the North Central Association

1956 – Fr. Tom Brown redecorates the chapel using Romanesque paintings

1957–1958 – Augustine Hall and Woods Hall built

1959–1960 – Centennial Hall built

1959 – Fr. Julian Woods begins elimination of Greek societies

1959 – Enrollment reaches 1,000 for the first time

1960 – Fraternities and sororities suppressed; reinstated in 1997

1962–1963 – Maintenance building constructed

1963 – Garner Hall opens

1964 – Friars' Hall opens with accommodations for sixty friars

1964 – Province builds Our Lady of Angels Seminary (now North Campus) and moves its college formation programs from Oak Brook, Illinois, and Cleveland, Ohio, to Quincy.

1964 – Soccer introduced

1965 – Garner Hall built

1965 – McHugh Theatre opens

1966 – Padua Hall opens

1966 – College Avenue closed

1966 – College begins fall semester in August

1966 – College wins first of eleven NAIA National Soccer Championships

1967 – Brenner Library constructed; includes specially designed climate-controlled rare book room

1970 – College Center (cafeteria) opens

1970 – Lind Street Hall (now Willer Hall) opens

1971 – Franciscan Provincial Council cedes control and ownership of the College to a combined Board of Trustees including friars and lay members

1974 – Radio station opens as WWQC (now WQUB)

1974 – Partnership Fund Campaign begins, ultimately collecting more than its five-year goal of $3.5 million

1975 – John Wood Community College opens under "common market" model

1978 – New soccer field built at North Campus (until then, soccer was played on the baseball half of QU-Stadium)

1979 – Faculty Senate organized

1983 – Carillon in tower dedicated

1983 – Women's soccer elevated to varsity status

1984 – Elm Street closed

1984 – Master of Business Administration (MBA) program begins

1984 – College acquires North Campus and QU-Stadium

1984 – College joins NCAA, Divisions I and II

1984 – Tower lighted at night

1985 – Fr. James Toal declares financial exigency and reduces faculty size

1985 – College wins NAIA National Softball Championship

1986 – Football reinstated as NCAA Division III sport

1989 – Renovation of Francis Hall begins (completed in 1994)

1991 – Master of Science in Education (M.S.Ed) degree approved

1991 – Lind Street closed

1991 – College acquires Franciscan Press

1993 – College renamed Quincy University

1994 – "Windows to the Future" sculpture dedicated

1994 – Tennis courts moved to Twentieth and Elm

1995 – Institute for Learning in Retirement begins (now POLIS: Pursuit of Learning in Society)

1995 – NCAA rule change requires that all varsity sports at Quincy be in the same Division

1997 – Fr. Eugene Kole, O.F.M. Conv. appointed as president; becomes first non-Observant branch friar (O.F.M.) to hold this position in University history

1998 – Official relationship between Quincy University and Blessing-Rieman College of Nursing established

2001 – Health and Fitness Center dedicated

2004 – Quincy University and John Wood Community College sign articulation agreement

2004 – Sr. Margaret Feldner, O.S.F. appointed as president; becomes first woman president in University history

2005 – Mart Heinen Softball Complex opens at North Campus (before this women played softball at Maranatha Field north of Quincy)

2005 – Master of Theological Studies (MTS) accredited by Higher Learning Commission (HLC)

2006 – Quincy University provides wireless Internet campus-wide

2008 – Robert A. Gervasi, Ph.D. assumes presidency; becomes first lay president in University history

2009 – New stained glass windows with lighting installed on the tower above Francis Hall; lighting ceremony kicks off 150th anniversary celebration

Conclusion: Education on the Periphery

MANY OF US WHO HAVE GONE TO SCHOOL IN, or come from, the centers of intellectual culture, experience the city of Quincy as a town on the periphery. People here often say that trends from the outside arrive late in Quincy.

Several things can be said about this. One is that, if Quincy is on the periphery, so is 90 percent of the world's population. While half of the world lives in cities, most of those people are as much on the periphery as anyone in rural America. If the values of college education are worth incarnating in every culture, the task of incarnating them in peripheral settings is at least as important as enjoying them in the center, and a lot more challenging. Therefore many of us stay in Quincy as people determined to create a blended environment through our outside experiences.

Quincy University has contributed much to the intellectual and cultural atmosphere of west-central Illinois. The College has had well-known national figures on campus; people such as John Kennedy, Bob Hope, John Philip Sousa, Walter Mondale, Mrs. Ronald Reagan, Richard Durbin, Everett Dirksen, Adlai Stevenson III, Studs Terkel, Buckminster Fuller, Arthur Schlesinger, Jr., Eugene McCarthy, Edward Kennedy, Bob Woodward, David Frost, Dick Gregory, Ralph Nader, Mortimer Adler, and Saul Alinsky. Years ago it seemed to me, while visiting my parents in Springfield, Illinois, that Springfield's *State Journal-Register* had far less coverage of national and international events than the Quincy *Herald-Whig*. I speculated that it was because Springfield at the time had no four-year college or university that its newspaper focused so much more on local affairs.

Another thing that can be said about Quincy is that people here do things for themselves. This little city, with its population of 40,000 in west-central Illinois, has an incredible array of cultural organizations. Quincy has, for example, its own community theatre, which stages professional-quality plays, including musicals, each year. It has an opera company and art galleries and a symphony and a symphonic chorus, a community band, and a park band, all maintained almost completely by unpaid volunteers. It has a large treasure of historic architecture, as well as a number of museums and historic sites. Each summer, it sponsors blues festivals in its central park, most of which can be attended free of charge, and the same park hosts an arts festival. We have Germanfest; the Quincy Cultural Festival; Riverfest, an event which showcases artists in the riverfront park area; and the Dogwood Festival and Parade, with dozens of entries representing every conceivable organization. We have the Veterans' Day Parade and the St. Patrick's Day Parade. When you live on the periphery, if you want something special, you have to create it yourself.

At the same time, Quincy and its surrounding rural towns experience many social obstacles facing rural America. Despite these barriers, the community continues to make efforts in providing resources overcoming these challenges. There are many active service organizations, such as Catholic Charities, the locally based "Ladies of Charity," Kiwanis, Exchange Club, and Rotary Club that contain men and women who are truly committed to serving those underprivileged. The local Salvation Army chapter is currently building a Ray & Joan Kroc Corps Community Center and the city has an active Human Rights Commission.

The do-it-yourself spirit shows itself in athletics. Quincy is known throughout the state of Illinois as a sports town, specifically in basketball, and is a place that produces statewide competitive teams from both its public and parochial schools. In a recent Great Lakes Valley Conference (GLVC) women's basketball tournament, Quincy University was the second smallest school from the dozen or more colleges in the tournament. Visiting teams in all sports marvel at the turnout for games here, compared to their experience in other places. The interest in athletics in Quincy is so great that, judging by the clippings carefully preserved in scrapbooks in the school archive, 90 percent of the press coverage of the College over the years deals with sports.

Other areas of Quincy University's history could be more fully developed. My story puts great emphasis on the Franciscan heritage of the school, as experienced by a friar. Untold numbers of faculty, staff, alumni, and friends over the years have had every bit as much dedication to the school and its values as any of the friars who have worked here. While many talented men and women have taught here for a while and then moved on, others equally talented have stayed, in good times and in bad. We have regularly produced highly successful graduates, who reported back, from their experience beyond Quincy, that what they got at Quincy made them as well prepared as any of their new peers for the challenges of a wider environment.

Education, like any other human enterprise, is continually changing. Optimists will say that it is "evolving," which suggests progress toward greater excellence.

The Franciscan Intellectual Tradition (capitalized because the phrase has become institutionalized in a series of conferences and publications) still awaits a convincing incarnation into the academy. By now, the friars have become older and less numerous, leaving the field open to younger scholars and teachers.

The sociological theory of "secularization," which dominated public thinking for a hundred years, predicted that religious colleges lose their distinctive religious heritage and instead retain their excellence as purely secular institutions. I believe, however, that our Catholic and Franciscan college will continue to create a vibrant atmosphere that will make original and creative contributions to public life and thought.

After 150 years, through all the ups and downs, Quincy University is still here, facing the future, but more importantly, educating the young, and not-so-young, men and women who continue to come to us. These men and women often do not know what they want, other than to make a decent life for themselves and their families. We can "edify" them today just as well as any of our predecessors could.

On his deathbed, St. Francis is supposed to have said, "Let us begin, for up to now we have done but little." That is our spirit now.

Index

About the Author

JOSEPH ZIMMERMAN, O.F.M. was born in Decatur, Illinois, entered the Franciscan Order in 1955, was ordained to the priesthood in 1962, earned a Ph.D. at Harvard, and taught sociology full-time at Quincy University from 1970 to 1998. Since then, he has combined teaching with various administrative roles within the University, including dean of faculty. He was responsible for implementing Quincy University's TAU degree-completion program for adult learners.

He has been actively involved in the Quincy community over the years and currently serves as a member of the governing board of the Franciscan Province of the Sacred Heart.

Teaching sociology was not his first choice for an occupation, and Quincy College was not where he intended to spend his life. But he chose to live as a friar in community, and to respond to God's call as expressed in the will of his friar brothers. He is at peace with his story, and looks forward to continuing that story, as it involves all the people that God sends into his life.